The best of Mrs BEETON'S Puddings & Desserts

The best of Mrs BEETON'S Puddings & Desserts

WEIDENFELD & NICOLSON

This edition produced for The Book People Ltd, Hall Wood Avenue, Haydock, St Helens WA11 9UL

First published in 2006 by the Orion Publishing Group Ltd
5 Upper St Martin's Lane
London
WC2H 9EA

Designed by seagulls and cbdesign
Index prepared by Chris Bell
Produced by Omnipress Ltd, Eastbourne
Printed in China

Contents

Jellies

Jellies make refreshing desserts after heavy meals.
Choose fruit or wine, strong black coffee,
or delicate milk jellies infused
with flavour.

FRESH LEMON JELLY

pared rind and juice of 4 lemons
20 ml / 4 tsp gelatine
100–175 g / 4–6 oz caster sugar

Put the lemon rind into a saucepan. Add 175 ml / 6 fl oz water and simmer for 5 minutes. Set aside until cool.

Place 75 ml / 3 fl oz water in a small bowl and sprinkle on the gelatine. Set aside for 15 minutes until the gelatine is spongy. Stand the bowl over a saucepan of hot water and stir the gelatine until it has dissolved completely. Stir a further 75 ml / 3 fl oz water into the dissolved gelatine. Remove the lemon rind from the cooled liquid and add the liquid to the gelatine mixture with the lemon juice and sugar to taste. Stir until the sugar has dissolved, heating gently if necessary.

Pour the mixture into four individual wetted moulds or a 750-ml / 1¼-pint mould and leave to set for about 1 hour.

SERVES FOUR

VARIATION

• **Fresh Orange Jelly** Use 2 oranges instead of lemons and reduce the amount of caster sugar to only 50 g / 2 oz.

MRS BEETON'S TIP

To turn out, or unmould, a jelly, run the tip of a knife around the top of the mould. Dip the mould into hot water for a few seconds, remove and dry it. Wet a serving plate and place upside down on top of the mould. Hold plate and mould together firmly and turn both over. Check that the mould is correctly positioned on the plate, sliding it into place if necessary. Shake gently and carefully lift off the mould.

ORANGE JELLY BASKETS

100 g / 4 oz sugar
6 oranges
2 lemons
40 g / 1½ oz gelatine

DECORATION
6 angelica strips
125 ml / 4 fl oz double cream

Put 500 ml / 17 fl oz water into a saucepan. Add the sugar. Pare the rind from three of the oranges. Add the rind to the pan and bring slowly to the boil. Leave to infuse for 10 minutes, keeping the pan covered.

Squeeze the juice from all the oranges and lemons; make up to 500 ml / 17 fl oz with water if necessary. Reserve the unpeeled orange halves for the baskets. Place 30 ml / 2 tbsp of the mixed citrus juice in a small bowl and sprinkle the gelatine on to the liquid. Set aside for 15 minutes until the gelatine is spongy. Stand the bowl over a saucepan of hot water and stir the gelatine until it has dissolved completely. Stir the remaining citrus juice and dissolved gelatine into the sugar syrup.

Remove any pulp from the 6 reserved orange halves and put the orange skins into patty tins to keep them supported. Strain the jelly into the orange shells; chill for about 2 hours until set.

Make handles from the angelica, keeping them in place by pushing the ends into the set jelly. Whip the cream in a bowl until stiff, then spoon into a piping bag. Decorate the baskets with the cream.

SERVES SIX

BLACKCURRANT JELLY

250 ml / 8 fl oz blackcurrant syrup
45 ml / 3 tbsp sugar
20 ml / 4 tsp gelatine

Heat the blackcurrant syrup and sugar in a saucepan, stirring until the sugar has dissolved. Set aside to cool.

Place 125 ml / 4 fl oz water in a small bowl and sprinkle the gelatine on to the liquid. Set aside for 15 minutes until the gelatine is spongy. Stand the bowl over a saucepan of hot water and stir the gelatine until it has dissolved completely. Stir in a further 125 ml / 4 fl oz cold water, then add the dissolved gelatine to the cooled syrup.

Pour the blackcurrant jelly into wetted individual moulds or a 600-ml / 1-pint mould and chill until set.

SERVES FOUR

APPLE JELLY

1 kg / 2¼ lb cooking apples
175 g / 6 oz sugar
2 cloves
grated rind and juice of 2 small lemons
40 g / 1½ oz gelatine

Wash the apples and cut them into pieces. Put them into a saucepan with the sugar, cloves, lemon rind and juice. Add 500 ml / 17 fl oz water. Cover, and cook until the apples are soft.

Place 60 ml / 4 tbsp water in a small bowl and sprinkle the gelatine on to the liquid. Set aside for 15 minutes until the gelatine is spongy. Stand the bowl over a saucepan of hot water and stir the gelatine until it has dissolved completely.

Rub the cooked apples through a sieve into a bowl and stir in the dissolved gelatine. Pour into a wetted 1.1-litre / 2-pint mould and chill until set.

SERVES FOUR TO SIX

VARIATION

• **Gooseberry Jelly** Use 1 kg / 2¼ lb prepared gooseberries instead of apples, and omit the cloves.

PORT WINE JELLY

25 ml / 5 tsp gelatine
50 g / 2 oz sugar
30 ml / 2 tbsp redcurrant jelly
250 ml / 8 fl oz port
few drops of red food colouring

Place 30 ml /2 tbsp water in a small bowl and sprinkle the gelatine on to the liquid. Set aside for 15 minutes until the gelatine is spongy. Stand the bowl over a saucepan of hot water and stir the gelatine until it has dissolved.

Combine the sugar and redcurrant jelly in a pan. Add 400 ml / 14 fl oz water and heat gently, stirring constantly, until all the sugar has dissolved.

Add the gelatine liquid to the syrup and stir in the port and food colouring. Pour through a strainer lined with a single thickness of scalded fine cotton or muslin into a wetted 900-ml / 1½-pint mould. Chill until set.

SERVES SIX

CLARET JELLY

4 lemons
150 g / 5 oz sugar
40 g / 1½ oz gelatine
whites and shells of 2 eggs
125 ml / 4 fl oz claret
few drops of red food colouring

Before you begin, scald a large saucepan, measuring jug, a bowl. a whisk and 900-ml / 1½-pint jelly mould in boiling water, as the merest trace of grease may cause cloudiness in the finished jelly.

Pare the rind from two of the lemons; squeeze the juice from all of them into the measuring jug. Make up to 125 ml / 4 fl oz with water, if necessary. Combine the lemon rind, lemon juice, sugar and gelatine in the large pan. Add 625 ml / 21 fl oz water.

Put the egg whites into the bowl; wash the shells in cold water, dry with absorbent kitchen paper and crush finely. Add the egg whites and crushed shells to the mixture in the pan and heat. whisking constantly until a good head of foam is produced. The mixture should be hot but not boiling. When the foam begins to form a crust, remove the whisk but continue to heat the liquid until the crust has risen to the top of the saucepan. Do not allow the liquid to boil.

Pour in the claret without disturbing the foam crust. Boil the liquid again until it reaches the top of the pan. Remove the saucepan from the heat. cover and let the contents settle in a warm place for 5 minutes. Meanwhile scald a jelly bag in boiling water and place it on a stand (see Mrs Beeton's Tip). Scald two large bowls; place one under the jelly bag.

Strain the settled, clear jelly through the hot jelly bag into the bowl. When all the jelly has passed through the bag, replace the bowl of jelly with the second scalded bowl and strain the jelly again, pouring it very carefully through the foam crust which covers the bottom of the bag and acts as a filter.

If the jelly is not clear when viewed in a spoon or glass, the filtering must be carried out again, but avoid doing this too many times, as repeated filtering will cool the jelly and cause some of it to stick to the cloth.

When the jelly is clear, add the colouring. Rinse the jelly mould in cold water. Pour the jelly into the wetted mould and chill until set.

SERVES SIX

MRS BEETON'S TIP

If you do not have a jelly bag and stand, improvise by tying the four corners of a perfectly clean, scalded cloth, to the legs of an upturned stool. Alternatively, line a large, scalded, metal sieve with muslin.

BLACK MAMBA

500 ml / 17 fl oz strong black coffee
50 g / 2 oz sugar
20 ml / 4 tsp gelatine
15 ml / 1 tbsp rum or liqueur
whipped cream to decorate

Set aside 30 ml / 2 tbsp coffee in a small bowl. Put the remaining coffee into a saucepan with the sugar and heat stirring, until the sugar has dissolved. Set aside to cool.

Sprinkle the gelatine on to the coffee in the small bowl. Set aside for 15 minutes until the gelatine is spongy. Stand the bowl over a saucepan of hot water and stir until the gelatine has dissolved. Add to the coffee syrup with the rum or liqueur.

Strain the mixture into a wetted 750-ml / 1¼-pint mould and chill until set. When ready to serve the jelly, turn out and decorate with whipped cream.

SERVES FOUR

MILK JELLY

500 ml / 17 fl oz milk
30 ml / 2 tbsp sugar
grated rind of 1 lemon
20 ml / 4 tsp gelatine

Put the milk, sugar and lemon rind into a saucepan. Heat, stirring, until the sugar has dissolved. Set aside to cool.

Place 60 ml / 4 tbsp water in a small bowl and sprinkle the gelatine on to the liquid. Set aside for 15 minutes until the gelatine is spongy. Stand the bowl over a saucepan of hot water and stir the gelatine until it has dissolved. Stir the gelatine mixture into the cooled milk, then strain into a bowl. Stir the mixture from time to time until it is the consistency of thick cream.

Pour the milk jelly into a wetted 750-ml / 1¼-pint mould and chill until set.

SERVES FOUR

VARIATIONS

- The jelly may be flavoured with vanilla, coffee or other essence, if liked. If coffee essence is used, substitute orange rind for the lemon. Omit the rind if peppermint flavouring is used.

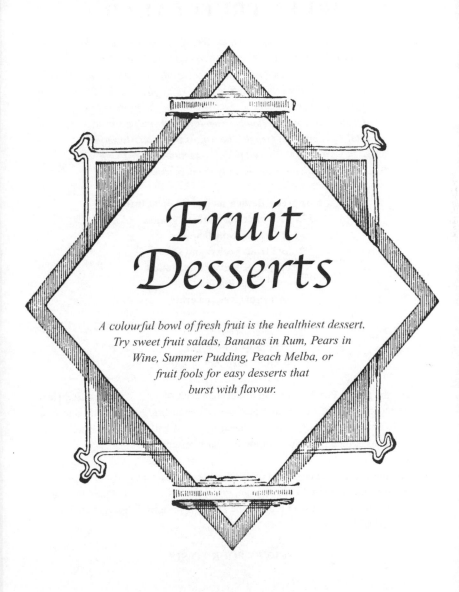

Fruit Desserts

*A colourful bowl of fresh fruit is the healthiest dessert.
Try sweet fruit salads, Bananas in Rum, Pears in
Wine, Summer Pudding, Peach Melba, or
fruit fools for easy desserts that
burst with flavour.*

GREEN FRUIT SALAD

A fruit salad, fresh, crisp and flavoursome, is the perfect ending
for a meal. Using shades of a single colour can be most effective.
Here the theme is green and white, but golden or red colours
can look equally attractive (see Red Fruit Salad, page 12).
There is no need to stick to the selection or the proportions
of fruit in the recipe; simply remember that you will need a
total of about 1 kg / 2¼ lb. The fruit is traditionally served
in syrup but fresh fruit juices, sometimes spiked with
alcohol, are equally popular today.

175 g / 6 oz green-fleshed melon, scooped into balls
175 g / 6 oz seedless green grapes
2 Granny Smith apples
2 kiwi fruit, peeled and sliced
2 greengages, halved and stoned
2 passion fruit
mint sprigs to decorate

SYRUP
175 g / 6 oz sugar
30 ml / 2 tbsp lemon juice

Make the syrup. Put the sugar in a saucepan with 450 ml / ¾ pint water. Heat gently, stirring until the sugar has dissolved, then bring to the boil and boil rapidly until the syrup has been reduced by about half. Add the lemon juice, allow to cool, then pour the syrup into a glass serving bowl.

When the syrup is quite cold, add the fruit. Leave the skin on the apples and either slice them or cut them into chunks. Cut the passion fruit in half and scoop out the pulp, straining it to remove the seeds, if preferred. Serve well chilled, decorated with mint.

SERVES FOUR TO SIX

ORANGE AND GRAPEFRUIT SALAD

Ortaniques would make a delicious addition to this salad.
These juicy citrus fruits are a cross between a tangerine and an orange.
Their thin skins make them very easy to peel and segment.

4 oranges
2 pink grapefruit

SYRUP
225 g / 8 oz sugar
30 ml / 2 tbsp orange liqueur

Using a vegetable peeler, remove the rind from 1 orange, taking care not to include any of the bitter pith. Cut the rind into strips with a sharp knife. Bring a small saucepan of water to the boil, add the orange strips and cook for 1 minute, then drain and set aside on absorbent kitchen paper.

Peel the remaining oranges and remove all the pith. Using a sharp knife, carefully cut between the segment membranes to remove the flesh. Work over a bowl to catch any juice, and squeeze out all the juice from the remaining pulp. Segment the grapefruit in the same way.

Make the syrup. Put the sugar in a pan with 200 ml / 7 fl oz water. Heat gently, stirring until the sugar has dissolved, then bring to the boil and boil rapidly, without stirring, until the syrup turns golden. Remove from the heat and carefully add the fruit juice and liqueur. Set aside to cool.

Arrange the citrus segments in concentric circles in a shallow serving dish or large quiche dish. Pour the caramel syrup over the top and chill thoroughly before serving.

SERVES SIX

RED FRUIT SALAD

Choose small strawberries, if possible, for this dessert, since they are juicier when left whole. Do not strip the redcurrants from the stalks.

225 g / 8 oz redcurrants
6 red plums, stoned and quartered
225 g / 8 oz strawberries, hulled
225 g / 8 oz raspberries, hulled
100 g / 4 oz slice watermelon, seeded and cubed

TO SERVE
Greek yogurt or clotted cream
caster sugar

Using a pair of kitchen scissors, neatly snip the redcurrants into small bunches.

Combine the plums, strawberries, raspberries and watermelon on a large platter. Arrange the redcurrants around or over the salad.

Serve as soon as possible, with yogurt or cream. Offer a bowl of caster sugar.

SERVES SIX

TROPICAL FRUIT SALAD

This fruit salad uses both fresh and canned fruits.

1 small pineapple
1 mango
1 x 312 g / 11 oz can lychees, drained
3 bananas, sliced
1 x 425 g / 15 oz can guava halves, drained
250 ml / 8 fl oz tropical fruit juice

Peel the pineapple, removing the eyes. Cut in half or quarters lengthways and cut out and discard the hard core. Cut the pineapple flesh into neat chunks and place in a serving dish.

Peel and slice the mango, discarding the stone. Add the mango flesh to the bowl along with the lychees, bananas and guavas. Pour over the tropical fruit juice and chill.

SERVES EIGHT

VARIATION

- Orange juice, spiked with a little rum, may be used instead of tropical fruit juice. Alternatively, try ginger wine.

MRS BEETON'S ORANGE SALAD

5 oranges
50 g / 2 oz caster sugar (or to taste)
2.5 ml / ½ tsp ground mixed spice
100 g / 4 oz muscatel raisins
60 ml / 4 tbsp brandy

Peel four oranges, removing all pith. Slice them, discarding the pips. Mix the sugar and spice in a bowl. Layer the orange slices in a serving dish, sprinkling each layer with the sugar mixture and raisins.

Squeeze the juice from the remaining orange and sprinkle it over the salad. Pour over the brandy, cover and leave to macerate for 24 hours before serving.

SERVES FOUR

PINEAPPLE AND KIRSCH SALAD

2 small pineapples
100 g / 4 oz black grapes
1 banana
1 pear
15 ml / 1 tbsp lemon juice
30–45 ml / 2–3 tbsp kirsch
sugar

Cut the pineapples in half lengthways. Cut out the cores, then scoop out the flesh, using first a knife, then a spoon, but taking care to keep the shells intact. Discard the cores, and working over a bowl to catch the juice, chop the flesh.

Add the pineapple flesh to the bowl. Halve the grapes and remove the pips. Add to the pineapple mixture. Peel and slice the banana; peel, core, and slice the pear. Put the lemon juice in a shallow bowl, add the pear and banana slices and toss both fruits before adding to the pineapple and grapes.

Mix all the fruit together, pour the kirsch over and sweeten to taste with the sugar. Pile the fruit back into the pineapple shells and chill until required.

SERVES FOUR

POIRES BELLE-HÉLÈNE

4 firm pears
250 ml / 8 fl oz Vanilla Ice Cream (page 37)

CHOCOLATE SAUCE
200 g / 7 oz plain chocolate, in squares
350 g / 12 oz sugar
salt
2.5 ml / ½ tsp vanilla essence

Make the sauce. Put the chocolate into a saucepan with the sugar, salt and vanilla essence. Add 250 ml / 8 fl oz water and heat gently, stirring, until the chocolate and sugar have melted and the mixture is smooth.

Peel the pears, cut them in half and remove the cores. Place a scoop or slice of ice cream in each of four dishes. Top with the pear halves and mask with the hot chocolate sauce.

SERVES FOUR

PLUMS WITH PORT

1 kg / 2¼ lb firm plums
100–150 g / 4–5 oz soft light brown sugar
150 ml / ¼ pint port

Set the oven at 150°C / 300°F / gas 2. Cut the plums neatly in half and remove the stones.

Put the plums into a baking dish or casserole, sprinkle with the sugar (the amount required will depend on the sweetness of the plums) and pour the port over the top.

Cover the dish securely with a lid or foil and bake for 45–60 minutes, or until the plums are tender. Serve hot or lightly chilled.

SERVES SIX

MICROWAVE TIP
Cook in a covered dish for
10-12 minutes on High,
stirring gently once or twice
during the cooking time.

STUFFED PEACHES
IN BRANDY

100 g / 4 oz sugar
150 ml / ¼ pint medium-dry or
slightly sweet white wine
30 ml / 2 tbsp brandy
6 large ripe peaches
125 ml / 4 fl oz double cream
50 g / 2 oz cut mixed peel
25 g / 1 oz blanched almonds, chopped

Put 250 ml / 8 fl oz water into a saucepan and add the sugar, wine and brandy. Place over low heat, stirring, until the sugar dissolves. Skin the peaches (see Microwave Tip), then poach them gently in the brandy syrup for 15 minutes. Leave in the syrup to cool completely.

Whip the cream in a bowl until it just holds its shape. Fold in the mixed peel and almonds. With a slotted spoon, remove the peaches from the cold syrup. Cut them in half and remove the stones. Put about 15 ml / 1 tbsp of the cream mixture in the hollow of 6 halves, then sandwich the peaches together again. Arrange in a shallow serving dish, and pour the syrup over the fruit. Chill until ready to serve.

SERVES SIX

MICROWAVE TIP

Prick the peach skins, then put
the fruit in a shallow dish.
Cover and microwave on High
for 1–1½ minutes. Allow to stand
for 5 minutes. The skins will
slip off easily.

PEARS IN WINE

100 g / 4 oz sugar
30 ml / 2 tbsp redcurrant jelly
1.5 cm / ¾ inch cinnamon stick
4 large ripe cooking pears (about 450 g / 1 lb)
250 ml / 8 fl oz red wine
25 g / 1 oz flaked almonds

Combine the sugar, redcurrant jelly and cinnamon stick in a saucepan wide enough to hold all the pears upright so that they fit snugly and will not fall over. Add 250 ml / 8 fl oz water and heat gently, stirring constantly, until the sugar and jelly have dissolved.

Peel the pears, leaving the stalks in place. Carefully remove as much of the core as possible without breaking the fruit. Stand the pears upright in the pan, cover, and simmer gently for 15 minutes.

Add the wine and cook, uncovered, for 15 minutes more. Remove the pears carefully with a slotted spoon, arrange them on a serving dish.

Remove the cinnamon stick from the pan and add the almonds. Boil the liquid remaining in the pan rapidly until it is reduced to a thin syrup. Pour the syrup over the pears and serve warm. This dessert can also be served cold. Pour the hot syrup over the pears, leave to cool, then chill before serving.

SERVES FOUR

FROSTED APPLES

oil for greasing
6 cooking apples (about 800 g / 1¾ lb)
30 ml / 2 tbsp lemon juice
100 g / 4 oz granulated sugar
15 ml / 1 tbsp fine-cut marmalade
2.5 cm / 1 inch cinnamon stick
2 cloves
2 egg whites
100 g / 4 oz caster sugar, plus extra
for dusting

DECORATION
125 ml / 4 fl oz double cream
glace cherries
angelica

Line a large baking sheet with greaseproof paper or non-stick baking parchment. Oil the lining paper. Set the oven at 180°C / 350°F / gas 4.

Wash, core and peel the apples, leaving them whole. Reserve the peelings. Brush the apples all over with the lemon juice to preserve the colour.

Combine the granulated sugar, marmalade, cinnamon stick, cloves and apple peelings in a large saucepan. Stir in 250 ml / 8 fl oz water. Heat gently, stirring occasionally, until the sugar and marmalade have melted, then boil for 2–3 minutes without stirring to make a thin syrup.

Place the apples in a baking dish and strain the syrup over them. Cover with a lid or foil and bake for about 30 minutes or until the apples are just tender. Lower the oven temperature to 120°C / 250°F / gas ½.

Using a slotted spoon, carefully remove the apples from the syrup, dry well on absorbent kitchen paper, then place on the prepared baking sheet.

Whisk the egg whites in a clean, grease-free bowl until they form stiff peaks, then gradually whisk in the caster sugar, a teaspoon at a time (see Mrs Beeton's Tip).

Coat each apple completely with the meringue, and dust lightly with caster sugar. Return to the oven and bake for about 1½ hours or until the meringue is firm and very lightly coloured. Remove from the oven and leave to cool.

In a bowl, whip the cream until it just holds its shape. Pile a spoonful on top of each apple and decorate with small pieces of cherry and angelica. Serve the apples on a bed of whipped cream in individual bowls, or with the cold baking syrup poured over them.

SERVES SIX

MRS BEETON'S TIP

If using an electric whisk to make the meringue, whisk in all the sugar. If whisking by hand, however, whisk in only half the sugar and fold in the rest.

BANANA BONANZA

4 bananas (about 450 g / 1 lb)
15 ml / 1 tbsp lemon juice
30 ml / 2 tbsp soft dark brown sugar
150 ml / ¼ pint soured cream
30 ml / 2 tbsp top-of-the-milk
grated chocolate to decorate

Mash the bananas with the lemon juice in a bowl. Stir in the sugar, soured cream and top-of-the-milk. Serve decorated with grated chocolate.

SERVES FOUR

BANANAS IN RUM

45 ml / 3 tbsp soft light brown sugar
2.5 ml / ½ tsp ground cinnamon
4 large bananas
25 g / 1 oz butter
45–60 ml / 3–4 tbsp rum
150 ml / ¼ pint double cream to serve

Mix the sugar and cinnamon in a shallow dish. Cut the bananas in half length-ways and dredge them in the sugar and cinnamon mixture.

Melt the butter in a frying pan and fry the bananas, flat side down, for 1–2 minutes or until lightly browned underneath. Turn them over carefully, sprinkle with any remaining sugar and cinnamon and continue frying.

When the bananas are soft but not mushy, pour the rum over them. Tilt the pan and baste the bananas, then ignite the rum; baste again. Scrape any caramelized sugar from the base of the pan and stir it into the rum sauce. Shake the pan gently until the flames die down.

Arrange the bananas on warmed plates, pour the rum sauce over the top and serve with cream.

SERVES FOUR

ORANGES IN CARAMEL SAUCE

6 oranges
200 g / 7 oz sugar
50–125 ml / 2–4 fl oz chilled orange juice

Using a vegetable peeler, remove the rind from 1 orange, taking care not to include any of the bitter pith. Cut the rind into strips with a sharp knife. Bring a small saucepan of water to the boil, add the orange strips and cook for 1 minute, then drain and set aside on absorbent kitchen paper.

Carefully peel the remaining oranges, leaving them whole. Remove the pith from all the oranges and place the fruit in a heatproof bowl.

Put the sugar in a saucepan with 125 ml / 4 fl oz water. Heat gently, stirring until the sugar has dissolved, then bring to the boil and boil rapidly, without stirring, until the syrup turns a golden caramel colour. Remove from the heat and carefully add the orange juice. Replace over the heat and stir until just blended, then add the reserved orange rind.

Pour the hot caramel sauce over the oranges and chill for at least 3 hours before serving.

SERVES SIX

FREEZER TIP

Cool the oranges quickly in the sauce, place in a rigid container, cover and freeze for up to 12 months. Remember to allow a little headspace in the top of the container, as the syrup will expand upon freezing. Thaw, covered, in the refrigerator for about 6 hours.

SUMMER PUDDING

This delectable dessert started life with the cumbersome name
of Hydropathic Pudding. It was originally invented for spa patients
who were forbidden rich creams and pastries. Vary the fruit filling
if you wish – blackberries or bilberries make very good additions –
but keep the total quantity of fruit at about 1 kg / 2¼ lb.

150 g / 5 oz caster sugar
225 g / 8 oz blackcurrants or redcurrants,
stalks removed
225 g / 8 oz ripe red plums, halved and stoned
1 strip of lemon rind
225 g / 8 oz strawberries, hulled
225 g / 8 oz raspberries, hulled
8–10 slices of day-old white bread,
crusts removed

Put the sugar into a saucepan with 60 ml / 4 tbsp water. Heat gently, stirring, until the sugar has dissolved. Add the black- or redcurrants, plums and lemon rind and poach until tender.

Add the strawberries and raspberries to the saucepan and cook for 2 minutes. Remove from the heat and, using a slotted spoon, remove the lemon rind.

Cut a circle from 1 slice of bread to fit the base of a 1.25-litre / 2¼-pint pudding basin. Line the base and sides of the basin with bread, leaving no spaces. Pour in the stewed fruit, reserving about 45–60 ml / 3–4 tbsp of the juice in a jug. Top the stewed fruit filling with more bread slices. Cover with a plate or saucer that exactly fits inside the basin. Put a weight on top to press the pudding down firmly. Leave in a cool place for 5–8 hours, preferably overnight.

Turn out carefully on to a plate or shallow dish to serve. If there are any places on the bread shell where the juice from the fruit filling has not penetrated, drizzle a little of the reserved fruit juice over. Serve with whipped cream or plain yogurt.

SERVES SIX

CHERRIES JUBILEE

This famous dish was created for Queen Victoria's Diamond Jubilee. It is often finished at the table, with the cherries and sauce kept warm in a chafing dish and the kirsch ignited and added at the last moment.

50 g / 2 oz sugar
450 g / 1 lb dark red cherries, stoned
10 ml / 2 tsp arrowroot
60 ml / 4 tbsp kirsch

Put the sugar in a heavy-bottomed saucepan. Add 250 ml / 8 fl oz water. Heat gently, stirring, until the sugar has dissolved, then boil steadily without stirring for 3–4 minutes to make a syrup. Lower the heat, add the cherries and poach gently until tender. Using a slotted spoon, remove the cherries from the pan and set them aside on a plate to cool.

In a cup, mix the arrowroot with about 30 ml / 2 tbsp of the syrup to a thin paste. Stir back into the pan. Bring to the boil, stirring constantly, until the mixture thickens. Remove from the heat.

Pile the cherries in a heatproof serving bowl. Pour the sauce over them. Heat the kirsch in a small saucepan or ladle. Ignite it, pour it over the cherries and serve at once.

SERVES FOUR

GOOSEBERRY FOOL

When elderflowers are available, try adding 2 heads, well washed and tied in muslin, to the gooseberries while poaching. Discard the muslin bags when the gooseberries are cooked.

575 g / 1¼ lb gooseberries, topped and tailed
150 g / 5 oz caster sugar
300 ml / ½ pint whipping cream

Put the gooseberries in a heavy-bottomed saucepan. Stir in the sugar. Cover the pan and cook the gooseberries over gentle heat for 10–15 minutes until the skins are just beginning to crack. Leave to cool.

Purée the fruit in a blender or food processor, or rub through a sieve into a clean bowl.

In a separate bowl, whip the cream until it holds its shape. Fold the cream gently into the gooseberry purée. Spoon into a serving dish or six individual glasses. Chill before serving.

SERVES SIX

VARIATIONS

- If a fruit is suitable for puréeing, it will make a creamy fool. Try rhubarb, apricots, red- or blackcurrants, raspberries or blackberries. Sieve the purée if necessary.

MICROWAVE TIP

Combine the gooseberries and sugar in a deep 1.2 litre / 2 pint dish. Cover lightly and cook for 6 minutes on High. Proceed as in the above recipe.

REDCURRANT AND RASPBERRY FOOL

225 g / 8 oz redcurrants
225 g / 8 oz raspberries
75–100 g / 3–4 oz caster sugar
15 ml / 1 tbsp cornflour
extra caster sugar for topping
25 g / 1 oz flaked almonds to decorate

Put the redcurrants and raspberries in a saucepan. Add 375 ml / 13 fl oz water and simmer gently for about 20 minutes or until very tender. Purée in a blender or food processor, then sieve the mixture to remove any seeds. Return the mixture to the clean pan.

Stir in caster sugar to taste. Put the cornflour into a cup and stir in about 30 ml / 2 tbsp of the purée. Bring the remaining purée to the boil.

Stir the cornflour mixture into the purée and bring back to the boil, stirring all the time until the fool thickens. Remove from the heat and spoon into six individual serving dishes. Sprinkle the surface of each fool with a little extra caster sugar to prevent the formation of a skin. Cool then chill thoroughly.

Top with the flaked almonds just before serving. Serve with whipped cream, Greek yogurt or fromage frais.

SERVES SIX

RHUBARB AND BANANA FOOL

450 g / 1 lb young rhubarb
75 g / 3 oz soft light brown sugar
piece of pared lemon rind
6 bananas
caster sugar (see method)
250 ml / 8 fl oz cold Cornflour Custard Sauce (page 220),
or lightly whipped double cream
ratafias, to decorate

Remove any strings from the rhubarb and cut the stalks into 2.5 cm / 1 inch lengths. Put into the top of a double saucepan and stir in the brown sugar and lemon rind. Set the pan over simmering water and cook for 10–15 minutes until the rhubarb is soft. Remove the lemon rind.

Meanwhile peel the bananas and purée in a blender or food processor. Add the rhubarb and process briefly until mixed. Alternatively, mash the bananas in a bowl and stir in the cooked rhubarb. Taste the mixture and add caster sugar, if necessary.

Fold the custard or cream into the fruit purée and turn into a serving bowl. Decorate with ratafias.

SERVES SIX TO EIGHT

MRS BEETON'S TIP

*If time permits, cook the rhubarb very slowly
overnight. Layer the fruit in a casserole, add the
sugar and lemon rind. Do not add any liquid.
Cover and bake at 110°C / 225°F / gas ¼.*

PAVLOVA

3 egg whites
150 g / 5 oz caster sugar
2.5 ml / ½ tsp vinegar
2.5 ml / ½ tsp vanilla essence
10 ml / 2 tsp cornflour
glacé cherries and angelica to decorate

FILLING
250ml / 8 fl oz double cream
caster sugar (see method)
2 peaches, skinned and sliced

Line a baking sheet with greaseproof paper or non-stick baking parchment. Draw a 20-cm / 8-inch circle on the paper and very lightly grease the greaseproof paper, if used. Set the oven at 150°C / 300°F / gas 2.

In a large bowl, whisk the egg whites until very stiff. Continue whisking, gradually adding the sugar until the mixture stands in stiff peaks. Beat in the vinegar, vanilla and cornflour.

Spread the meringue over the circle, piling it up at the edges to form a rim, or pipe the circle and rim from a piping bag fitted with a large star nozzle.

Bake for about 1 hour or until the pavlova is crisp on the outside and has the texture of marshmallow inside. It should be pale coffee in colour. Leave to cool then carefully remove the paper. Put the pavlova on a large serving plate.

Make the filling by whipping the cream in a bowl with caster sugar to taste. Add the sliced peaches and pile into the cold pavlova shell. Decorate with glacé cherries and angelica and serve as soon as possible.

SERVES FOUR

PEACH MELBA

Escoffier's original recipe, created for Dame Nellie Melba,
consisted of fresh peaches poached in vanilla syrup
and arranged in the centre of a bowl of vanilla ice cream.
Cold Melba Sauce was poured over the peaches and
the bowl containing the dessert was presented on
a dish of crushed ice. The version that follows is the
one that is more often served today.

500 ml / 17 fl oz Vanilla Ice Cream (page 37)
6 canned peach halves
125 ml / 4 fl oz double cream

MELBA SAUCE
575 g / 1¼ lb fresh raspberries
150 g / 5 oz icing sugar

Make the Melba Sauce. Put the raspberries in a sieve over a heatproof bowl. Using a wooden spoon, crush them against the sides of the sieve to extract as much of the juice as possible. Stir the sugar into the purée and place the bowl over a saucepan of simmering water. Stir for 2–3 minutes to dissolve the sugar. Cool the sauce, then chill until required.

Place a scoop or slice of ice cream in each of six sundae dishes. Cover each portion with a peach half. Coat with the Melba Sauce.

In a bowl, whip the cream until stiff. Spoon into a piping bag and pipe a large rosette on top of each portion. Serve at once.

SERVES SIX

DANISH APPLE CAKE

1 kg / 2¼ lb cooking apples
150 g / 5 oz dried white breadcrumbs
75 g / 3 oz sugar
100–125 g / 4–4½ oz butter

DECORATION
300 ml / ½ pint whipping cream
red jam, melted

Set the oven at 180°C / 350°F / gas 4. Place the apples on a baking sheet and bake for 1 hour. When cool enough to handle, remove the peel and core from each apple; purée the fruit in a blender or food processor or rub through a sieve into a bowl.

In a separate bowl, mix the breadcrumbs with the sugar. Melt the butter in a frying pan, add the crumb mixture and fry until golden.

Place alternate layers of crumbs and apple purée in a glass dish, starting and finishing with crumbs.

Whip the cream in a bowl and put into a piping bag fitted with a large star nozzle. Decorate the top of the apple cake with cream rosettes and drizzle a little melted red jam over the top. Chill lightly before serving.

SERVES FOUR TO SIX

DRIED FRUIT COMPOTE

100 g / 4 oz dried apricots
100 g / 4 oz prunes
100 g / 4 oz dried figs
50 g / 2 oz dried apple rings
30 ml / 2 tbsp liquid honey
2.5 cm / 1 inch cinnamon stick
2 cloves
pared rind and juice of ½ lemon
50 g / 2 oz raisins
50 g / 2 oz flaked almonds, toasted

Combine the apricots, prunes and figs in a bowl. Add water to cover. Put the apples in separate bowl with water to cover and leave both bowls to soak overnight.

Next day, place the honey in a saucepan with 600 ml / 1 pint water. Add the cinnamon stick, cloves and lemon rind. Bring to the boil. Stir in the lemon juice.

Drain both bowls of soaked fruit. Add the mixed fruit to the pan, cover and simmer for 10 minutes. Stir in the drained apples and simmer for 10 minutes more, then add the raisins and simmer for 2–3 minutes. Discard the cinnamon, cloves and lemon rind.

Spoon the compote into a serving dish and sprinkle with the almonds. Serve warm or cold.

SERVES SIX

MICROWAVE TIP

There is no need to presoak the dried fruit. Make the honey syrup in a large bowl, using 450 ml/ ¾ pint water. Microwave on High for about 4 minutes, then stir in all the dried fruit with the cinnamon, cloves and lemon rind. Cover and cook on High for 15–20 minutes or until all the fruit is soft. Stir several times during cooking, each time pressing the fruit down into the syrup.

Iced Desserts

Twinkling water ices and sorbets, ice creams and bombes
are popular with all ages and at all occasions.
Whether you choose simple or luxurious,
rich or low-calorie, you'll make the
perfect summer treat.

LEMON WATER ICE

6 lemons

2 oranges

SYRUP

350 g / 12 oz caster sugar

5 ml / 1 tsp liquid glucose

Turn the freezing compartment or freezer to the coldest setting about 1 hour before making the water ice.

Make the syrup. Put the sugar in a heavy-bottomed saucepan with 250 ml / 8 fl oz water. Dissolve the sugar over a gentle heat stirring occasionally. Bring to the boil and boil steadily, without stirring, for about 10 minutes or to a temperature of 110°C / 225°F. Remove any scum from the surface.

Strain the syrup into a large bowl and stir in the liquid glucose. Pare the rind very thinly from. the lemons and oranges and add to the bowl of syrup. Cover and set aside to cool.

Squeeze the fruit and add the juice to the cold syrup mixture. Strain through a nylon sieve into a suitable container for freezing.

Cover the container closely and freeze until half-frozen (when ice crystals appear around the edge of the mixture). Beat the mixture thoroughly, scraping off any crystals. Replace the cover and freeze until solid. Return the freezer to the normal setting.

Transfer the water ice to the refrigerator about 15 minutes before serving, to allow it to soften and 'ripen'. Serve in scoops in individual dishes or glasses.

SERVES SIX

RASPBERRY WATER ICE

450 g / 1 lb ripe raspberries
juice of 2 lemons

SYRUP
225 g / 8 oz caster sugar
3.75 ml / ¾ tsp liquid glucose

Turn the freezing compartment or freezer to the coldest setting about 1 hour before making the water ice.

Make the syrup. Put the sugar in a heavy-bottomed saucepan with 175 ml / 6 fl oz water. Dissolve the sugar over gentle heat without stirring. Bring the mixture to the boil and boil gently for about 10 minutes or until the mixture registers 110°C / 225°F on a sugar thermometer. Remove the scum as it rises in the pan.

Strain the syrup into a large bowl and stir in the liquid glucose. Cover and cool. Purée the raspberries in a blender or food processor, or rub through a sieve into a bowl. Strain, if necessary, to remove any seeds. Stir in the lemon juice. Stir the mixture into the syrup, then pour into a suitable container for freezing.

Cover the container closely and freeze until half-frozen (when ice crystals appear around the edge of the mixture). Beat the mixture thoroughly, scraping off any crystals. Replace the cover and freeze until solid. Return the freezer to the normal setting.

Transfer the water ice to the refrigerator about 15 minutes before serving, to allow it to soften and 'ripen'. Serve in scoops in individual dishes or glasses.

SERVES SIX

MANDARIN WATER ICE

50 g / 2 oz lump sugar
6 mandarins
225 g / 8 oz caster sugar
3.75ml / ¾ tsp liquid glucose
2 lemons
2 oranges

Turn the freezing compartment or freezer to the coldest setting about 1 hour before making the water ice.

Rub the sugar lumps over the rind of the mandarins to extract some of the zest. Put the sugar lumps in a heavy-bottomed saucepan with the caster sugar and 300 ml / ½ pint water.

Dissolve the sugar over gentle heat without stirring. Bring the mixture to the boil and boil gently for about 10 minutes or until the mixture registers 110°C / 225°F on a sugar thermometer. Remove the scum as it rises in the pan.

Strain the syrup into a large bowl and stir in the liquid glucose. Pare the rind very thinly from 1 lemon and 1 orange and add to the bowl of syrup. Cover and set aside to cool.

Squeeze all the fruit and add the juice to the cold syrup mixture. Strain through a nylon sieve into a suitable container. Cover the container closely and freeze until half-frozen (when ice crystals appear around the edge of the mixture). Beat the mixture thoroughly, scraping off any crystals. Replace the cover and freeze until solid. Return the freezer to the normal setting.

Transfer the water ice to the refrigerator about 15 minutes before serving, to allow it to soften and 'ripen'. Serve in scoops in individual dishes or glasses.

SERVES SIX TO EIGHT

PINEAPPLE SORBET

200 g / 7 oz lump sugar
250 ml / 8 fl oz pineapple juice
2 egg whites

Turn the freezing compartment or freezer to the coldest setting about 1 hour before making the sorbet.

Put the sugar in a heavy-bottomed saucepan with 500 ml / 17 fl oz water. Dissolve the sugar over gentle heat, without stirring. Bring the mixture to the boil and boil gently for about 10 minutes or until the mixtures registers 110°C / 225°F on a sugar thermometer. Remove the scum as it rises in the pan. Strain into a bowl, cover and leave to cool.

Add the pineapple juice to the syrup and pour into a suitable container for freezing. Cover the container closely and freeze until half-frozen.

In a clean, grease-free bowl whisk the egg whites until stiff. Beat the sorbet mixture until smooth, scraping off any ice crystals. Fold in the egg whites, replace the cover on the bowl and freeze. The mixture should be firm enough to scoop; it will not freeze hard. Return the freezer to the normal setting.

Serve straight from the freezer, either in individual dishes or glasses, or in scoops in a decorative bowl.

SERVES SIX

LEMON SORBET

10 ml / 2 tsp gelatine
150 g / 5 oz caster sugar
2.5 ml / ½ tsp grated lemon rind
250 ml / 8 fl oz lemon juice
2 egg whites

Turn the freezing compartment or freezer to the coldest setting about 1 hour before making the sorbet.

Place 30 ml / 2 tbsp water in a small bowl and sprinkle the gelatine on to the liquid. Set aside for 15 minutes until the gelatine is spongy. Stand the bowl over a pan of hot water; stir the gelatine until it has dissolved.

Put the sugar in a heavy-bottomed saucepan with 200 ml / 7 fl oz water. Dissolve the sugar over gentle heat, without stirring. Bring the mixture to the boil and boil gently for about 10 minutes. Stir the dissolved gelatine into the syrup, with the lemon rind and juice. Cover and cool.

Pour the cool syrup mixture into a suitable container for freezing, cover closely and freeze until half-frozen.

In a clean, grease-free bowl whisk the egg whites until stiff. Beat the sorbet mixture until smooth, scraping off any ice crystals. Fold in the egg whites, replace the cover and freeze. The mixture should be firm enough to scoop; it will not freeze hard. Return the freezer to the normal setting.

Serve straight from the freezer, in dishes, glasses or lemon shells.

SERVES SIX TO EIGHT

VANILLA ICE CREAM

30 ml / 2 tbsp custard powder
500 ml / 17 fl oz milk
100 g / 4 oz caster sugar
125 ml / 4 fl oz double cream
5 ml / 1 tsp vanilla essence

Turn the freezing compartment or freezer to the coldest setting about 1 hour before making the ice cream.

In a bowl, mix the custard powder to a cream with a little of the milk. Bring the remaining milk to the boil in a saucepan, then pour it into the bowl stirring constantly. Return the custard mixture to the clean pan and simmer, stirring all the time, until thickened. Stir in the sugar, cover closely with dampened grease-proof paper and set aside to cool.

In a large bowl, whip the cream to soft peaks. Add the cold custard and vanilla essence. Spoon into a suitable container for freezing. Cover the container closely and freeze until half-frozen (when ice crystals appear around the edge of the mixture). Beat the mixture until smooth, scraping off any crystals. Replace the cover and freeze until firm. Return the freezer to the normal setting.

Transfer the ice cream to the refrigerator about 15 minutes before serving, to allow it to soften and 'ripen'. Serve in scoops in individual dishes or in a large decorative bowl.

SERVES SIX

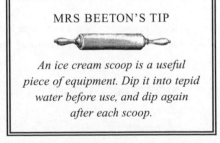

MRS BEETON'S TIP

An ice cream scoop is a useful piece of equipment. Dip it into tepid water before use, and dip again after each scoop.

RICH VANILLA ICE CREAM

**500 ml / 17 fl oz milk
3 eggs
175 g / 6 oz caster sugar
250 ml / 8 fl oz double cream
5 ml / 1 tsp vanilla essence**

Turn the freezing compartment or freezer to the coldest setting about 1 hour before making the ice cream.

In a saucepan, bring the milk to just below boiling point. Put the eggs into a bowl with 100 g / 4 oz of the sugar. Mix well then stir in the scalded milk. Strain the custard mixture into a heavy-bottomed saucepan or a heatproof bowl placed over a saucepan of simmering water. Alternatively, use a double saucepan, but make sure the water does not touch the upper pan.

Cook the custard over very gentle heat for 15–25 minutes, stirring all the time with a wooden spoon, until the custard coats the back of the spoon. Strain into a bowl, cover closely with damp greaseproof paper and cool.

In a large bowl, whip the cream to soft peaks. Add the cold custard, vanilla essence and remaining sugar. Stir lightly. Spoon into a suitable container for freezing.

Cover the container closely and freeze until half-frozen (when ice crystals appear around the edge of the mixture). Beat the mixture until smooth, scraping off any crystals. Replace the cover and freeze until firm. Return the freezer to the normal setting.

Transfer the ice cream to the refrigerator about 15 minutes before serving, and allow it to soften and 'ripen'. Serve in scoops in individual dishes or in a large decorative bowl.

SERVES SIX TO EIGHT

BROWN BREAD ICE CREAM

150 g / 5 oz fresh brown breadcrumbs
3 egg whites
100 g / 4 oz caster sugar
350 ml / 12 fl oz double cream

Turn the freezing compartment or freezer to the coldest setting about 1 hour before making the ice cream.

Set the oven at 120°C / 250°F / gas ½. Spread the breadcrumbs on a baking sheet and bake in the oven until golden brown, stirring occasionally. Set aside until cool.

In a clean, grease-free bowl whisk the egg whites until stiff. Gradually whisk in the caster sugar. In a second bowl, whip the cream to soft peaks. Fold the breadcrumbs and whipped cream into the whisked egg whites; spoon into a 1.1-litre / 2-pint pudding basin. Cover and freeze until firm. Return the freezer to the normal setting.

Invert the ice cream on a serving plate while still frozen. Allow it to soften and 'ripen' in the refrigerator for about 15 minutes before serving.

SERVES SIX TO EIGHT

MRS BEETON'S TIP

If an ice or ice cream is to be made by hand, rather than in a sorbetière or ice cream churn, it is helpful to freeze it in a container which allows for it to be beaten. If there is room in your freezer or freezing compartment, use a deep bowl or box which can be securely closed. A rigid plastic bowl is ideal, since the finished ice or ice cream can be stored in the same container. If your freezing compartment is shallow, or if you wish to freeze the mixture particularly quickly, use a shallow container such as an ice tray, and tip the contents into a chilled bowl for beating.

CARAMEL ICE CREAM

750 ml / 1¼ pints milk
3 eggs, plus 12 egg yolks
175 g / 6 oz caster sugar
50 g / 2 oz lump sugar
100 ml / 3 fl oz single cream

Turn the freezing compartment or freezer to the coldest setting about 1 hour before making the ice cream.

Heat the milk in a heavy-bottomed saucepan until just below boiling point. Beat the eggs and egg yolks with the caster sugar in a large bowl until thick and white, then add the hot milk, stirring well. Return the mixture to the clean pan and cook over gentle heat, stirring constantly, until the custard thickens. Do not allow it to boil. Pour the thickened custard into a large heatproof bowl and keep it hot over a saucepan of simmering water.

Put the lump sugar into a small heavy-bottomed pan. Add a few drops of water and heat gently until dissolved, then boil until the syrup is a deep golden colour. Remove from the heat, carefully add the cream and beat gently. Return the pan to the heat. As soon as the mixture starts to rise in the pan, stir it into the hot custard. Cover closely with dampened greaseproof paper and cool.

Spoon the cold mixture into a suitable container for freezing. Cover the container closely and freeze until half-frozen (when ice crystals appear around the edge of the mixture). Beat the mixture until smooth, scraping off any crystals. Replace the cover and freeze until firm. Return the freezer to the normal setting.

Transfer the ice cream to the refrigerator about 15 minutes before serving, to allow it to soften and 'ripen'. Serve in scoops in individual dishes or in a large bowl.

SERVES EIGHT TO TEN

RICH CHOCOLATE ICE CREAM

4 egg yolks
50 g / 2 oz caster sugar
250 ml / 8 fl oz single cream
100 g / 4 oz plain chocolate, in squares
125 ml / 4 fl oz double cream
5 ml / 1 tsp vanilla essence

Turn the freezing compartment or freezer to the coldest setting about 1 hour before making the ice cream.

Combine the egg yolks and caster sugar in a deep bowl and beat together until very thick. Put the single cream in a saucepan and bring slowly to the boil. Pour the cream over the yolks and sugar, stirring well. Return the mixture to the clean pan. Cook, stirring, until the custard thickens. Do not allow it to boil. Pour the thickened custard into a heatproof bowl and keep hot over a pan of simmering water.

Put the chocolate in a heatproof bowl and add 65 ml / 2½ fl oz water. Bring a saucepan of water to the boil, remove it from the heat, and set the bowl over the hot water until the chocolate has melted. Stir, then add the chocolate mixture to the hot custard; mix lightly. Cover closely with dampened greaseproof paper and cool.

In a bowl, whip the double cream until thick. Fold it into the cool chocolate custard, with the vanilla essence. Spoon into a suitable container for freezing. Cover the container closely and freeze until half-frozen (when ice crystals appear around the edge of the mixture). Beat the mixture until smooth. Replace the cover and freeze until firm. Return the freezer to the normal setting.

Transfer the ice cream to the refrigerator about 15 minutes before serving, to allow it to soften and 'ripen'.

SERVES SIX

GINGER ICE CREAM

125 ml / 4 fl oz milk
3 egg yolks
75 g / 3 oz caster sugar
75 g / 3 oz preserved ginger in syrup
60 ml / 4 tbsp ginger syrup (from the jar of preserved ginger)
10 ml / 2 tsp ground ginger
250 ml / 8 fl oz double cream

Turn the freezing compartment or freezer to the coldest setting about 1 hour before making the ice cream.

In a saucepan, bring the milk to just below boiling point. Put the egg yolks into a bowl with 25 g / 1 oz of the sugar. Mix well, then stir in the scalded milk. Return the mixture to the clean pan and cook gently, stirring constantly, until the custard coats the back of a wooden spoon. Do not allow it to boil. Cover the custard closely with dampened greaseproof paper and set aside to cool.

Dice the preserved ginger. Heat the syrup in a small saucepan and stir ground ginger until dissolved.

In a large bowl, whip the cream until stiff. Add the custard, diced ginger, syrup mixture and remaining sugar. Mix lightly. Spoon into a suitable container for freezing. Cover the container closely and freeze until half-frozen (when ice crystals appear around the edge of the mixture). Beat the mixture until smooth, scraping off any crystals. Replace the cover and freeze until firm. Return the freezer to the normal setting.

Transfer the ice cream to the refrigerator about 15 minutes before serving, to allow it to soften and 'ripen'. Serve in scoops in individual dishes or in a large decorative bowl.

SERVES SIX

MOCHA ICE CREAM

50 g / 2 oz caster sugar
30 ml / 2 tbsp instant coffee powder
150 g / 5 oz plain chocolate, in squares
3 egg yolks
250 ml / 8 fl oz double cream

Turn the freezing compartment or freezer to the coldest setting about 1 hour before making the ice cream.

Mix the sugar and coffee powder in a saucepan. Add 30 ml / 2 tbsp water and bring to the boil. Boil for 1 minute, then remove from the heat and add the chocolate. When the chocolate has melted, stir lightly, then set the pan aside.

When the chocolate mixture is cool, stir in the egg yolks. In a bowl, whip the cream to soft peaks. Fold in the chocolate mixture.

Spoon into a suitable container for freezing. Cover the container closely with foil; freeze until half-frozen (when ice crystals appear around the edge of the mixture). Tip the mixture into a bowl and beat until smooth, scraping off any crystals. Freeze until firm. Return the freezer to the normal setting.

Transfer the ice cream to the refrigerator about 15 minutes before serving, to allow it to soften and 'ripen'. Serve in scoops in individual dishes or in a large bowl.

SERVES FOUR

COFFEE ICE CREAM

45 ml / 3 tbsp instant coffee powder
300 ml / ½ pint double cream
75 g / 3 oz caster sugar

Turn the freezing compartment or freezer to the coldest setting about 1 hour before making the ice cream.

Pour 60 ml / 4 tbsp boiling water into a cup, add the instant coffee and stir until dissolved. Set aside until cool.

Whip the cream in a bowl until stiff. Stir in the sugar and fold in the dissolved coffee. Spoon into a suitable container for freezing. Cover the container closely and freeze until half-frozen (when ice crystals appear around the edge of the mixture). Beat the mixture until smooth, scraping off any crystals. Replace the cover and freeze until firm. Return the freezer to the normal setting.

Transfer the ice cream to the refrigerator about 15 minutes before serving, to allow it to soften and 'ripen'. Serve in individual dishes or in a large bowl.

SERVES FOUR

LEMON ICE CREAM

8 egg yolks
200 g / 7 oz caster sugar
juice of 2 lemons
250 ml / 8 fl oz double cream

Turn the freezing compartment or freezer to the coldest setting about 1 hour before making the ice cream.

In a bowl, beat the egg yolks until very thick. Add the caster sugar and beat again. Stir in the lemon juice.

Whip the cream to soft peaks in a deep bowl, then add carefully to the egg and sugar mixture. Spoon into a suitable container for freezing. Cover the container closely and freeze until half-frozen (when ice crystals appear around the edge of the mixture). Beat the mixture until smooth, scraping off any crystals. Replace the cover and freeze until firm. Return the freezer to the normal setting.

Transfer the ice cream to the refrigerator about 15 minutes before serving, to allow it to soften and 'ripen'. Serve in scoops in individual dishes or in a large decorative bowl.

SERVES SIX

COTTAGE YOGURT ICE CREAM

This is a good choice for slimmers.
Serve it with fresh strawberries or raspberries.

225 g / 8 oz plain cottage cheese
125 ml / 4 fl oz thick plain yogurt
30 ml / 2 tbsp liquid honey

Turn the freezing compartment or freezer to the coldest setting about 1 hour before making the ice cream.

Sieve the cheese into a bowl. Gently stir in the yogurt and honey. Spoon into a suitable container for freezing, allowing at least 2.5 cm / 1 inch headspace. Leave to stand for 30 minutes.

Cover the container closely and freeze until ice crystals appear around the edge of the mixture. Beat the mixture until smooth, scraping off any crystals. Replace the cover and freeze until firm. Return the freezer to the normal setting.

If left in the freezer, the ice cream will get progressively harder. To obtain the right consistency it will need to be thawed for 2–4 hours at room temperature, then returned to the freezer for about 30 minutes.

SERVES FOUR

STRAWBERRY LICK

400 g / 14 oz ripe strawberries, hulled
15 ml / 1 tbsp granulated sugar
125 ml / 4 fl oz milk
250 ml / 8 fl oz double cream
2 egg yolks
150 g / 5 oz caster sugar
5 ml / 1 tsp lemon juice
red food colouring

Turn the freezing compartment or freezer to the coldest setting about 1 hour before making the ice cream. Rub the strawberries through a nylon sieve into a bowl. Stir in the granulated sugar and set aside.

Combine the milk and cream in a saucepan and bring to just below boiling point. Beat the egg yolks with the caster sugar until thick and creamy, and stir in the milk and cream.

Return the custard mixture to the clean pan and simmer, stirring all the time, until thickened. Pour into a large bowl and stir in the strawberry purée and lemon juice. Tint pale pink with the food colouring.

Spoon the mixture into a suitable container for freezing. Cover the container closely and freeze until half-frozen (when ice crystals appear around the edge of the mixture). Beat the mixture until smooth, scraping off any crystals. Replace the cover and freeze until firm. Return the freezer to the normal setting.

Transfer the ice cream to the refrigerator about 15 minutes before serving, to allow it to soften and 'ripen'. Serve in scoops in individual dishes or a large bowl.

SERVES SIX

BOMBE TORTONI

*This is absurdly easy to make, yet it makes an impressive
finale for a dinner party.*

**300 ml / ½ pint double cream
150 ml / ¼ pint single cream
50 g / 2 oz icing sugar, sifted
2.5 ml / 1 tsp vanilla essence
2 egg whites
100 g / 4 oz hazelnut biscuits or ratafias, crushed
30 ml / 2 tbsp sherry**

Turn the freezing compartment or freezer to the coldest setting about 1 hour
before making the bombe. Lightly oil a 1.25-litre / 2¼-pint bombe mould or
pudding basin.

Combine the creams in a large bowl and whip until thick, adding half the icing
sugar. Add the vanilla essence.

In a clean, grease-free bowl whisk the egg whites until stiff. Fold in the remaining icing sugar.

Lightly fold the meringue mixture into the whipped cream. Stir in the hazelnut
biscuits and sherry. Spoon the mixture into the prepared mould.

Put the lid on the bombe mould or cover the basin with foil. Freeze until firm,
then return the freezer to the normal setting. To turn out, dip the mould or basin
in cold water, and invert on to a chilled serving dish. Transfer to the refrigerator 15 minutes before serving to allow the ice cream to soften and 'ripen'.

SERVES SIX TO EIGHT

VARIATIONS

- Try crushed ginger biscuits with coffee liqueur instead of sherry, or crumbled meringue with cherry brandy.

BOMBE CZARINE

1 quantity Vanilla Ice Cream (page 37)

FILLING
125 ml / 4 fl oz double cream
25 g / 1 oz icing sugar, sifted
2 egg whites
5 ml / 1 tsp kummel, or liqueur of own choice

Turn the freezing compartment or freezer to the coldest setting about 1 hour before making the bombe. Chill 2 bowls; a 1.4-litre / 2½-pint pudding basin or bombe mould, and a smaller 600-ml / 1-pint bowl.

Make the vanilla ice cream and freeze until half-frozen (when ice crystals appear around the edge of the mixture). Beat the mixture until smooth, scraping off any crystals.

Spoon a layer of the vanilla ice cream into the chilled mould. Centre the smaller bowl inside the mould, with its rim on a level with the top of the mould. Fill the space between the outer mould and the inner bowl with vanilla ice cream. Cover the mould and freeze until firm. Reserve any remaining ice cream in the freezer.

Meanwhile prepare the filling. In a bowl, whip the cream with half the sugar. Put the egg whites in a second, grease-free bowl and whisk until stiff. Fold in the remaining sugar. Carefully mix the cream and egg whites and add the liqueur. Chill lightly.

When the vanilla ice cream is firm, remove the bowl from the centre of the mould (filling it with warm water if necessary to dislodge it). Fill the centre of the ice cream mould with the liqueur mixture, covering it with any remaining ice cream.

Put on the lid on the bombe mould or cover the basin with foil. Freeze until firm. Return the freezer to the normal setting.

To turn out, dip the mould or basin in cold water, and invert on to a chilled serving dish. Transfer to the refrigerator 15 minutes before serving, to allow the ice cream to soften and 'ripen'.

SERVES SIX TO EIGHT

VARIATIONS

- **Bombe Zamora** Use coffee ice cream instead of vanilla to line the mould, and flavour the filling with curaçao.
- **Bombe Nesselrode** As above, but add 60 ml / 4 tbsp chestnut purée to the filling, which should be flavoured with kirsch instead of kummel or any other liqueur.

JAPANESE PLOMBIÈRE

A plombière is an ice cream mixture containing almonds
or chestnuts. It may be frozen in a decorative mould but is more
often scooped into balls and piled up to form a pyramid.
It is often served with a sauce poured over the top.

50 g / 2 oz apricot jam
few drops of lemon juice
8 egg yolks
100 g / 4 oz caster sugar
500 ml / 17 fl oz single cream
2.5 ml / ½ tsp vanilla essence
100 g / 4 oz ground almonds
250 ml / 8 fl oz double cream
100 g / 4 oz almond macaroons, crushed
12 ratafias to decorate

Turn the freezing compartment or freezer to the coldest setting about 1 hour before making the ice cream.

Make an apricot marmalade by boiling the apricot jam in a small saucepan with a few drops of lemon juice until thick. Keep a little aside for decoration and sieve the rest into a bowl.

Combine the egg yolks and caster sugar in a deep bowl and beat together until very thick. Put the single cream in a saucepan and bring slowly to the boil. Pour the cream over the yolks and sugar, stirring well. Return the mixture to the clean pan. Cook, stirring constantly, until the custard thickens. Do not allow it to boil. Pour the thickened custard into a large bowl and stir in the sieved apricot marmalade, the vanilla essence and the ground almonds. Cover closely with dampened greaseproof paper and cool.

In a bowl, whip the double cream to the same consistency as the custard. Fold it into the custard, with the crushed macaroons. Spoon the mixture into a suitable container for freezing (a bowl that is deep enough to allow the ice cream to be scooped is ideal). Freeze the mixture until firm.

To serve, scoop the ice cream into balls and arrange them as a pyramid on a chilled plate. Drizzle the reserved apricot marmalade over the top and decorate with the ratafias.

SERVES SIX TO EIGHT

MICROWAVE TIP

The apricot marmalade may be prepared in a small bowl in the microwave. It will only require about 30 seconds on High. Reheat it, if necessary, before pouring it over the ice cream pyramid.

VANILLA PLOMBIÈRE

1 quantity Vanilla Ice Cream (page 37)
125 ml / 4 fl oz double cream
50 g / 2 oz flaked almonds

Make the ice cream and freeze it until firm in a suitable container.

In a bowl, whip the cream to soft peaks. Beat the ice cream until smooth, scraping off any ice crystals, then fold in the whipped cream and almonds. Spoon into a suitable container, cover and freeze the ice cream until firm.

If the ice cream has been made in a mould or basin, turn it out on to a chilled plate and transfer it to the refrigerator about 15 minutes before serving, to allow it to soften and 'ripen'. If a plastic box or bowl has been used, scoop the ice cream into balls and form these into a pyramid on a dish.

SERVES SIX

NESSELRODE PUDDING

24 chestnuts
250 ml / 8 fl oz milk
4 egg yolks
150 g / 5 oz caster sugar
250 ml / 8 fl oz double cream
vanilla essence
50 g / 2 oz glace cherries

Turn the freezing compartment or freezer to the coldest setting about 1 hour before making the pudding.

Using a sharp knife, make a small slit in the rounded side of the shell of each chestnut. Bring a saucepan of water to the boil, add the chestnuts and boil for 5 minutes. Drain. Peel the chestnuts while still very hot. Return them to the clean pan and add 125 ml / 4 fl oz of the milk. Simmer gently until the chestnuts are tender, then rub them through a fine sieve into a bowl.

Put the egg yolks in a bowl and beat lightly. Pour the rest of the milk into a saucepan and bring to just below boiling point. Pour the milk on to the egg yolks, stirring well. Return the mixture to the clean pan and simmer, stirring constantly, until the custard thickens. Do not let it boil.

Remove the custard from the heat and stir in the chestnut purée and the sugar. Leave until cool.

In a bowl, whip half the cream to soft peaks. Add to the chestnut mixture along with a few drops of vanilla essence. Pour into a a suitable bowl for freezing, cover and freeze until half-frozen (when ice crystals appear around the edge of the mixture).

Meanwhile rinse the cherries, pat dry on absorbent kitchen paper, and chop finely. In a bowl, whip the remaining cream until stiff.

Beat the ice cream mixture until smooth, scraping off the crystals. Stir in the chopped cherries and fold in the whipped cream. Return to the freezer until almost set, stirring the mixture frequently. Press into a 750-ml / 1¼-pint mould, cover, and return to the freezer until the mixture is firm. Return the freezer to the normal setting.

Transfer the pudding to the refrigerator about 15 minutes before serving, to allow it to soften and 'ripen'.

SERVES SIX

CHOCOLATE FREEZER PUDDING

100 g / 4 oz butter, plus extra for greasing
100 g / 4 oz drinking chocolate powder
100 g / 4 oz ground almonds
100 g / 4 oz caster sugar
1 egg, beaten
100 g / 4 oz Petit Beurre biscuits
whipped cream to decorate

Grease a 20-cm / 8-inch square baking tin. In a mixing bowl. cream the butter and chocolate powder together. Work in the ground almonds.

Put the sugar into a heavy-bottomed saucepan. Add 30 ml / 2 tbsp water and heat gently until the sugar has melted. Set aside to cool.

Gradually add the syrup to the ground almond mixture, working it in well. Add the egg in the same way and beat the mixture until light and creamy.

Break the biscuits into small pieces and fold into the pudding mixture. Spoon into the prepared tin, pressing the mixture down well. Cover and freeze until firm.

To serve the pudding, thaw at room temperature for 45 minutes, then turn out on a serving dish. Decorate with whipped cream.

SERVES TEN TO TWELVE

BAKED ALASKA

*For this popular dessert to be a success it must
be assembled and cooked at the last minute.
Make sure that the ice cream is as hard as possible,
that the ice cream and sponge are completely coated
in meringue, and that the oven has reached the
recommended temperature. Watch the Baked Alaska
closely as it cooks, and remove it from the oven as
soon as the swirls of meringue are golden brown.*

**2 egg whites
150 g / 5 oz caster sugar
1 quantity Vanilla Ice Cream (page 37)**

CAKE
**butter for greasing
2 eggs
50 g / 2 oz caster sugar
few drops of vanilla essence
50 g / 2 oz plain flour, sifted
30 ml / 2 tbsp melted butter, cooled**

Make the cake several hours before you intend to serve the dessert. Line and grease a 20-cm / 8-inch sandwich cake tin. Set the oven to 180°C / 350°F / gas 4.

Combine the eggs, sugar and vanilla essence in a heatproof bowl. Place over a saucepan of simmering water and whisk until the mixture is thick, pale lemon in colour, and has doubled in bulk. This will take 6–8 minutes. Remove the bowl from the heat and continue to beat until cooled and very thick.

Working swiftly and lightly, fold in the flour, then the butter. Spoon into the prepared tin and bake for 25–30 minutes or until cooked through and firm to the touch. Cool the cake on a wire rack.

When almost ready to serve the Baked Alaska, set the oven at 230°C / 450°F / gas 8. Put the egg whites in a clean, grease-free bowl and whisk until very stiff. gradually whisking in half the sugar. Fold in the remaining sugar.

Place the cold cake on an ovenproof plate and pile the ice cream on to it, leaving a 1-cm / ½-inch clear border all around. Cover quickly with the meringue, making sure that both the ice cream and the cake are completely covered. Draw the meringue into swirls, using the blade of a knife or a palette knife.

Immediately put the Alaska into the oven and bake for 3–4 minutes until the meringue is just beginning to brown. Serve at once.

SERVES SIX TO EIGHT

VARIATIONS

- The dessert may be made with a slab of sponge cake and a family brick of bought ice cream. Fresh or drained canned fruit may be laid on the sponge base before the ice cream and meringue is added.

MRS BEETON'S TIP

Wash and dry half an egg shell, pop a sugar cube into it, and soak the sugar cube liberally in brandy. Just before serving the dessert, set the egg shell firmly on the top of the meringue and ignite the brandy for a spectacular effect.

SPUMA GELATO PAOLO

30 ml / 2 tbsp gelatine
250 g / 9 oz caster sugar
100 ml / 3 fl oz Marsala
30 ml / 2 tbsp brandy or orange liqueur
1 whole egg, plus 3 yolks
finely grated rind of 1 lemon
90 ml / 6 tbsp lemon juice
300 ml / ½ pint double cream
3 drops of orange essence
150 g / 5 oz peeled orange segments

Turn the freezing compartment or freezer to the coldest setting about 1 hour before making the ice cream. In a bowl. mix the gelatine with 150 g / 5 oz of the caster sugar to form jelly crystals. Stir in 150 ml / ¼ pint boiling water and stir until the crystals have dissolved. Set aside until cool.

Warm the Marsala and brandy gently in a small saucepan. Combine the egg and egg yolks in a large heatproof bowl. Whisk for at least 8 minutes until light and fluffy, then place over a pan of simmering water.

Add the warmed Marsala mixture and lemon rind to the bowl and stir in 60 ml / 4 tbsp lemon juice. Cook the custard mixture, whisking constantly, until it is thick enough to coat a spoon. Stir in the cooled gelatine mixture.

Whip the cream to soft peaks. Fold in the remaining sugar, then fold into the Marsala custard. Add the orange essence with the remaining lemon juice. Spoon into a wetted 1-litre / 1¾-pint mould and freeze for at least 4 hours. Return the freezer to the normal setting.

To serve, unmould on to a plate and thaw at room temperature for 15 minutes. Decorate with orange segments.

SERVES SIX

Soufflés
& Mousses

*A perfect hot dessert soufflé is the crowning glory of
any meal. Light yet luscious, chilled soufflés
and mousses are equally impressive,
prepare-ahead alternatives.*

HOT SOUFFLÉS

To ensure soufflé success, you must be confident and well organised. The flavoured base mixture should be prepared in advance, ready for the egg whites to be whisked and folded-on just before cooking. Timing is crucial, so work out a timetable and plan exactly when you intend to finish preparing the soufflé and place it in the oven. When cooked, the soufflé should be taken immediately to the table and served.

You will need an ovenproof, straight-sided soufflé dish or individual soufflé or ramekin dishes. These should be buttered. For sweet soufflés, dishes may be sprinkled with a little caster sugar to help the mixture cling to the sides as it rises.

For easy removal from the oven, stand individual dishes on a baking sheet once they are prepared. As soon as the dish, or dishes, have been filled with mixture, quickly wash and dry your hands and run your thumb around the inside edge of the dish, cleaning away the mixture, to create a gutter. This ensures that the mixture rises evenly and high instead of sticking to the top edge of the dish, which would make it dome and crack.

VANILLA SOUFFLÉ

butter for greasing
40 g / 1½ oz butter
40 g / 1½ oz plain flour
250 ml / 8 fl oz milk
4 eggs, separated, plus 1 white
50 g / 2 oz caster sugar
2.5 ml /½ tsp vanilla essence
caster or icing sugar for dredging

Grease a 1-litre / 1¾-pint soufflé dish. Set the oven at 180°C / 350°F / gas 4.

Melt the butter in a saucepan, stir in the flour and cook slowly for 2–3 minutes without colouring, stirring all the time. Add the milk gradually and beat until smooth. Cook for 1–2 minutes more, still stirring.

Remove from the heat and beat hard until the sauce comes away cleanly from the sides of the pan. Cool slightly and put into a bowl. Beat the yolks into the flour mixture one by one. Beat in the sugar and vanilla essence.

In a clean, grease-free bowl, whisk all the egg whites until stiff. Using a metal spoon, stir 1 spoonful of the whites into the mixture to lighten it, then fold in the rest until evenly distributed. Spoon into the prepared dish and bake for 45 minutes until well risen and browned.

Dredge with caster or icing sugar and serve immediately from the dish, with Jam Sauce (page 236).

SERVES FOUR TO SIX

VARIATIONS

- **Almond Soufflé** Add 100 g / 4 oz ground almonds, 15 ml / 1 tbsp lemon juice and a few drops of ratafia essence to the mixture before adding the egg yolks. Reduce the sugar to 40 g / 1½ oz. Omit the vanilla essence.
- **Coffee Soufflé** Add 30 ml / 2 tbsp instant coffee dissolved in a little hot water before adding the egg yolks, or use 125 ml / 4 fl oz strong black coffee and only 125 ml / 4 fl oz milk. Omit the vanilla essence.
- **Ginger Soufflé** Add a pinch of ground ginger and 50 g / 2 oz chopped preserved stem ginger before adding the egg yolks. Omit the vanilla essence. Serve each portion topped with double cream and ginger syrup.
- **Lemon Soufflé** Add the thinly grated rind and juice of 1 lemon before adding the egg yolks. Omit the vanilla essence. Serve with Rich Lemon Sauce (page 216).
- **Liqueur Soufflé** Add 30 ml / 2 tbsp Cointreau, kirsch or curaçao instead of vanilla essence and make as for Soufflé au Grand Marnier (page 60). Serve with sweetened cream flavoured with the liqueur.
- **Orange Soufflé** Thinly pare the rind of 2 oranges. Put in a saucepan with the milk and bring slowly to the boil. Remove from the heat, cover, and leave to stand for 10 minutes, then remove the rind. Make up the sauce using the flavoured milk. Reduce the sugar to 40 g / 1½ oz and omit the vanilla essence. Add the strained juice of ½ orange.
- **Praline Soufflé** Dissolve 30–45 ml / 2–3 tbsp almond Praline (see Mrs Beeton's Tip, page 73) in the milk before making the sauce, or crush and add just before the egg yolks. Omit the vanilla essence.

- **Soufflé au Grand Marnier** Add 30–45 ml / 2–3 tbsp Grand Marnier to the orange soufflé mixture. Serve with an orange sauce made by boiling 125 ml / 4 fl oz orange juice and a few drops of liqueur with 50 g / 2 oz caster sugar until syrupy. Add very fine strips of orange rind to the mixture.
- **Soufflé Ambassadrice** Crumble 2 almond macaroons; soak them in 30 ml / 2 tbsp rum with 50 g / 2 oz chopped blanched almonds. Stir into a vanilla soufflé mixture.
- **Soufflé Harlequin** Make up 2 half quantities of soufflé mixture in different flavours, eg chocolate and vanilla, or praline and coffee. Spoon alternately into the dish.
- **Soufflé Rothschild** Rinse 50 g / 2 oz mixed glacé fruit in hot water to remove any excess sugar. Chop the fruit and soak it in 30 ml / 2 tbsp brandy or kirsch for 2 hours. Make up 1 quantity vanilla soufflé mixture. Put half the vanilla soufflé mixture into the dish, add the fruit, and then the rest of the soufflé mixture.
- **Soufflé Surprise** Crumble 3 sponge fingers or almond macaroons into a bowl. Soak the biscuits in 30 ml / 2 tbsp Grand Marnier or Cointreau. Add 30 ml / 2 tbsp of the same liqueur to an orange soufflé mixture. Put half the mixture into the dish, sprinkle the biscuits on top, and add the rest of the soufflé mixture.

HOT FRUIT SOUFFLÉS

For fruit-flavoured soufflés a thick, sweet purée is added to the basic Vanilla Soufflé (page 58). It is important that the purée should have a strong flavour, otherwise the taste will not be discernible. If extra purée is added, the soufflé will be heavy and will not rise.

- **Apple Soufflé** Add 125 ml / 4 fl oz thick sweet apple purée, 15 ml / 1 tbsp lemon juice, and a pinch of powdered cinnamon to the soufflé before adding the egg yolks. Dust the soufflé with cinnamon before serving.
- **Apricot Soufflé** Before adding the egg yolks, add 125 ml / 4 fl oz thick fresh apricot purée and 15 ml / 1 tbsp lemon juice. If using canned apricots – 1 x 397 g / 14 oz can yields 125 ml / 4 fl oz purée – use half milk and half can syrup for the sauce. A purée made from dried apricots makes a delicious soufflé.

- **Pineapple Soufflé** Before adding the egg yolks, add 125 ml / 4 fl oz crushed pineapple or 75 g / 3 oz chopped fresh pineapple, and make the sauce using half milk and half pineapple juice.
- **Raspberry Soufflé** Before adding the egg yolks, add 125 ml / 4 fl oz raspberry purée – 1 x 397 g / 14 oz can yields 125 ml / 4 fl oz purée – and 10 ml / 2 tsp lemon juice.
- **Strawberry Soufflé** Before adding the egg yolks, add 125 ml / 4 fl oz strawberry purée. Make the sauce using half milk and half single cream. Add a little pink food colouring, if necessary.

SEMOLINA SOUFFLÉ

Banish all thoughts of semolina as something thick and porridge-like.
This soufflé is light and lovely.

butter for greasing
pared rind of ½ lemon
400 ml / 14 fl oz milk
50 g / 2 oz semolina
50 g / 2 oz caster sugar
3 eggs, separated

Grease a 1-litre / 1¾-pint soufflé dish. Set the oven at 180°C / 350°F / gas 4.

Combine the lemon rind and milk in a saucepan and bring to the boil. Immediately remove from the heat and leave to stand for 10 minutes. Remove the rind and sprinkle in the semolina. Cook for 2–3 minutes, stirring all the time, until the semolina mixture thickens. Stir in the sugar and leave to cool.

Beat the egg yolks into the semolina mixture one by one. In a clean, grease-free bowl, whisk the egg whites until stiff, and fold into the semolina mixture. Put into the prepared dish and bake for 45 minutes. Serve at once, with Apricot Sauce (page 228) or Redcurrant Sauce (page 214).

SERVES FOUR

SWEET SOUFFLÉ OMELETTE

Soufflé omelettes are quick and easy to make – the perfect finale
for the busy cook. Fill simply with 30 ml / 2 tbsp warmed jam
or try any of the exciting fillings that follow.

2 eggs, separated
5 ml / 1 tsp caster sugar
few drops of vanilla essence
15 ml / 1 tbsp unsalted butter or margarine
icing sugar for dredging

In a large bowl, whisk the yolks until creamy. Add the sugar and vanilla essence with 30 ml / 2 tbsp water, then whisk again. In a clean, grease-free bowl, whisk the egg whites until stiff and matt.

Place an 18-cm / 7-inch omelette pan over gentle heat and when it is hot, add the butter or margarine. Tilt the pan to cover the base. Pour out any excess.

Fold the egg whites into the yolk mixture until evenly distributed, using a metal spoon. Be very careful not to overmix, as it is the air incorporated in the frothy whites that causes the omelette to rise. Heat the grill to moderate.

Pour the egg mixture into the omelette pan, level the top very lightly, and cook for 1–2 minutes over moderate heat until the omelette is golden brown on the underside and moist on top. (Use a palette knife or spatula to lift the edge of the omelette to look underneath.)

Put the pan under the grill for 5–6 minutes until the omelette is risen and lightly browned on the top. The texture of the omelette should be firm yet spongy. Remove from the heat as soon as it is ready, as over-cooking tends to make it tough. Run a palette knife gently round the edge and underneath to loosen it. Make a mark across the middle at right angles to the pan handle but do not cut the surface. Put the chosen filling on one half, raise the handle of the pan and double the omelette over. Turn gently on to a warm plate, dredge with icing sugar and serve at once.

SERVES ONE

FILLINGS

- **Apricot Omelette** Add the grated rind of 1 orange to the egg yolks. Spread 30 ml / 2 tbsp warm, thick apricot purée over the omelette.
- **Cherry Omelette** Stone 100 g / 4 oz dark cherries, or use canned ones. Warm with 30 ml / 2 tbsp cherry jam and 15 ml / 1 tbsp kirsch. Spread over the omelette.
- **Creamy Peach Omelette** Stone and roughly chop 1 ripe peach, then mix it with 45 ml / 3 tbsp cream cheese. Add a little icing sugar to taste and mix well until softened. Spread over the omelette.
- **Jam Omelette** Warm 45 ml / 3 tbsp fruity jam and spread over the omelette.
- **Lemon Omelette** Add the grated rind of ½ lemon to the egg yolks. Warm 45 ml / 3 tbsp lemon curd with 10 ml / 2 tsp lemon juice, and spread over the omelette.
- **Orange Chocolate Omelette** Warm 15 ml / 1 tbsp orange marmalade and mix with 30 ml / 2 tbsp chocolate spread. Spread over the omelette.
- **Raspberry Omelette** Spread 30 ml / 2 tbsp warm, thick, raspberry purée or Melba Sauce (page 28) over the omelette.
- **Rum Omelette** Add 15 ml / 1 tbsp rum to the egg yolks.
- **Strawberry Omelette** Hull 5 ripe strawberries and soak in a bowl with a little kirsch. Mash slightly with icing sugar to taste. Put in the centre of the omelette.
- **Surprise Omelette** Put ice cream into the centre of the omelette before folding. Work quickly to prevent the ice cream from melting and serve the omelette immediately.

SPECIAL EFFECTS

- **Flambé Omelette** Warm 30 ml / 2 tbsp rum or brandy. Put the cooked omelette on to a warm plate, pour the warmed spirit round it, ignite, and serve immediately.
- **Branded Omelettes** Soufflé omelettes are sometimes 'branded' for a special occasion. A lattice decoration is marked on the top using hot skewers. Heat the pointed ends of three metal skewers until red-hot. When the omelette is on the plate, dredge with icing sugar. Protecting your hand in an oven glove, quickly press the hot skewers, one at a time, on to the sugar, holding them there until the sugar caramelizes. Make a diagonal criss-cross design. Each skewer should make two marks if you work quickly.

COLD SOUFFLÉS

*Cold soufflés are easier to make than hot ones
and may be prepared in advance; the difference being
that gelatine is used instead of heat to set the eggs.*

PREPARING A COLD SOUFFLÉ DISH

Using a piece of string, measure the height of the dish and its circumference. Cut a strip from two thicknesses of greaseproof paper or non-stick baking parchment that exceeds the height of the dish by 7.5 cm / 3 inches and is long enough to go right around the dish with an overlap. Tie the paper around the dish with string. If the dish has sloping sides or a projecting rim, secure the paper above and below the rim with gummed tape. Make sure the paper has no creases and forms a neat, round shape. When the soufflé has set, untie the string and carefully peel the paper away, running the blade of a knife between paper and soufflé to ensure that the mixture standing above the rim keeps its shape.

MRS BEETON'S TIP

*The size of the soufflé dish is crucial, since
the mixture must 'rise' above it. If in doubt as
to the capacity of the dish, measure by pouring
in 500 ml / 17 fl oz water. If the dish is slightly
too small, do not worry, since the crown
will merely be a little taller. A larger dish,
however, will not be suitable.*

MILANAISE SOUFFLÉ

15 ml / 1 tbsp gelatine
3 eggs, separated
grated rind and juice of 2 lemons
100 g / 4 oz caster sugar
125 ml / 4 fl oz double cream

DECORATION
finely chopped nuts or cake crumbs
whipped double cream (optional)
crystallized lemon slices
angelica

Prepare a 500-ml / 17-fl oz soufflé dish (see Mrs Beeton's Tip page 64) and stand it on a plate for easy handling.

Place 45 ml / 3 tbsp water in a small bowl and sprinkle the gelatine on to the liquid. Set aside for 15 minutes until the gelatine is spongy. Stand the bowl over a pan of hot water and stir the gelatine until it has dissolved completely. Cool slightly.

Combine the egg yolks, lemon rind and juice, and sugar in a heatproof bowl and stand over a saucepan of hot water set over low heat. Do not let the water boil or touch the bowl. Whisk the mixture for 10–15 minutes until thick and pale, then remove from the heat and continue whisking until cool. Fold a little of the yolk mixture into the cooled gelatine, then whisk this into the rest of the yolk mixture. Put in a cool place until the mixture starts to set.

In a bowl, whip the cream to soft peaks. Using a large metal spoon, fold into the yolk mixture until evenly blended. Whisk the egg whites in a clean, grease-free bowl until stiff, then fold into the mixture. Tip the soufflé gently into the prepared dish and refrigerate until set.

Carefully remove the paper from the crown of the soufflé and decorate the sides with chopped nuts or cake crumbs. Pipe whipped cream on top, if liked, and decorate with crystallized lemon slices and small pieces of angelica.

SERVES FOUR

VARIATIONS

In each of the variations below, omit the lemon rind and juice.

- **Cold Chocolate Soufflé** Whisk the yolks with 30 ml / 2 tbsp water and 75 g / 3 oz caster sugar. Melt 75 g / 3 oz grated plain chocolate over a saucepan of hot water. Add to the yolk mixture with the dissolved gelatine and whisk well.
- **Cold Orange Soufflé** Whisk the yolks with the finely grated rind and juice of 2 oranges and use 75 g / 3 oz caster sugar only. Add 30 ml / 2 tbsp Grand Marnier or orange curaçao, if liked. Dissolve the gelatine in a mixture of 15 ml / 1 tbsp water and 30 ml / 2 tbsp lemon juice. Decorate the soufflé with crystallized orange slices, nuts and cream.
- **Cold Praline Soufflé** Make 75 g / 3 oz Praline (see Mrs Beeton's Tip, page 73) and crush it. Dissolve 5 ml / 1 tsp instant coffee in 30 ml / 2 tbsp hot water, and add 30 ml / 2 tbsp cold water. Whisk the liquid with the yolks. Add 50 g / 2 oz of the crushed praline to the mixture with the whipped cream. Decorate with the remaining praline and additional cream.

COLD FRUIT SOUFFLÉS

The recipe below uses raspberries but other fresh, frozen or canned soft fruits, such as strawberries, blackcurrants or blackberries, may be substituted to produce a strongly flavoured soufflé.

- **Cold Raspberry Soufflé** Soften the gelatine in 45 ml / 3 tbsp of strained fruit syrup from 1 x 440 g / 15½ oz can of raspberries. Add 15 ml / 1 tbsp lemon juice and 150 ml / ¼ pint sieved fruit to the yolk mixture (this can be made up with a little strained syrup, if necessary). Use only 75 g / 3 oz sugar and 100 ml / 3½ fl oz double cream. Decorate the sides of the soufflé with desiccated coconut, and the top with whipped cream and raspberries.
- **Cold Apricot Soufflé** Dried apricots make a delicious soufflé. Soak 50 g / 2 oz overnight in enough water to cover. Tip into a saucepan and simmer for 15–20 minutes until tender, then purée in a blender or food processor. Soften the gelatine in a mixture of 15 ml / 1 tbsp water and 30 ml / 2 tbsp lemon juice. Add the apricot purée (made up to 150 ml / ¼ pint with water, if necessary) and proceed as in the recipe above.

MILK CHOCOLATE SOUFFLÉ

10 ml / 2 tsp gelatine
2 eggs, separated
50 g / 2 oz caster sugar
150 ml / ¼ pint evaporated milk, chilled
75 g / 3 oz milk chocolate

DECORATION
whipped cream
grated milk chocolate

Prepare a 500-ml / 17-fl oz soufflé dish (see page 64) and stand it on a plate for easy handling.

Place 30 ml / 2 tbsp water in a small bowl and sprinkle the gelatine onto the liquid. Set aside for 15 minutes until the gelatine is spongy. Stand the bowl over a pan of hot water and stir the gelatine until it has dissolved completely. Cool slightly.

Combine the egg yolks and sugar in a heatproof bowl and stand over a saucepan of hot water set over low heat. Do not let the water boil or touch the bowl. Whisk the mixture for 5–10 minutes until thick and pale, then remove the bowl from the heat.

In a bowl, whisk the chilled evaporated milk until thick, then whisk into the egg yolk mixture. Melt the chocolate on a plate over simmering water and whisk into the mixture. Fold a little of the chocolate mixture into the cooled gelatine, then whisk this into the rest of the chocolate mixture. Put in a cool place until the mixture starts to set.

Whisk the egg whites in a clean, grease-free bowl until stiff, then fold into the mixture. Tip the soufflé gently into the prepared dish and refrigerate for about 2 hours until set.

Carefully remove the paper from the crown of the soufflé and decorate with whipped cream and grated chocolate.

SERVES FOUR

CHOCOLATE MOUSSE

150 g / 5 oz plain chocolate, grated
4 eggs, separated
vanilla essence

DECORATION
whipped cream
chopped walnuts

Put the grated chocolate into a large heatproof bowl with 30 ml / 2 tbsp water. Stand over a saucepan of simmering water until the chocolate melts. Remove from the heat and stir the mixture until smooth.

Beat the egg yolks into the chocolate with a few drops of vanilla essence. In a clean, grease-free bowl, whisk the egg whites until fairly stiff, then fold gently into the chocolate mixture until evenly blended. Pour into 4 individual dishes and refrigerate for 1–2 hours until set. Decorate with whipped cream and chopped walnuts just before serving.

SERVES FOUR

VARIATIONS

- **Mocha Mousse** Dissolve 5 ml / 1 tsp instant coffee in 30 ml / 2 tbsp hot water and stir into the chocolate along with the egg yolks and vanilla essence.
- **Choc-au-Rhum Mousse** Add 15 ml / 1 tbsp rum to the mixture. Alternatively, use brandy, Grand Marnier or Tia Maria.
- **White Mousse** Use white chocolate, melting it into 30 ml / 2 tbsp single cream instead of water.

CHOCOLATE AND ORANGE MOUSSE

100 g / 4 oz plain chocolate, grated
60 ml / 4 tbsp fresh orange juice
10 ml / 2 tsp gelatine
3 eggs, separated
vanilla essence
100 ml / 3½ fl oz double cream

DECORATION
whipped cream
coarsely grated plain chocolate

Put the grated chocolate into a large heatproof bowl with the orange juice. Sprinkle the gelatine on to the liquid. Set aside for 15 minutes until the gelatine is spongy. Stand the bowl over a saucepan of simmering water until the chocolate melts and the gelatine dissolves. Remove from the heat and stir until smooth.

Beat the egg yolks into the chocolate mixture with a few drops of vanilla essence. Whip the cream in a separate bowl until it just holds its shape, then fold into the mixture.

In a clean, grease-free bowl, whisk the egg whites until fairly stiff, then fold gently into the chocolate mixture until blended. Pour into a wetted 750-ml / 1¼-pint mould or deep serving bowl and refrigerate for about 2 hours until set. Turn out, if necessary, and decorate with whipped cream and grated chocolate.

SERVES FOUR

MICROWAVE TIP
*Dissolve the chocolate and
gelatine in the orange juice
in a suitable bowl on
High for 2–3 minutes.*

MANGO MOUSSE

1 kg / 2¼ lb ripe mangoes
90 ml / 6 tbsp fresh lime juice
100 g / 3½ oz caster sugar
15 ml / 1 tbsp gelatine
2 egg whites
pinch of salt
100 ml / 3½ fl oz double cream
15 ml / 1 tbsp light rum

Peel the fruit and cut the flesh off the stones. Purée with the lime juice in a blender or food processor (see Mrs Beeton's Tip). When smooth, blend in the sugar, then scrape the mixture into a bowl with a rubber spatula.

Place 45 ml / 3 tbsp water in a small bowl. Sprinkle the gelatine on to the liquid. Set aside for 15 minutes until the gelatine is spongy. Stand the bowl over a pan of hot water and stir the gelatine until it has dissolved completely. Cool slightly, then stir into the mango purée.

In a clean, grease-free bowl, whisk the egg whites with the salt until they form fairly stiff peaks. Stir 15 ml / 1 tbsp of the egg whites into the purée to lighten it, then fold in the rest.

Lightly whip the cream and rum together in a separate bowl, then fold into the mango mixture as lightly as possible. Spoon into a serving bowl. Refrigerate for about 3 hours until set.

SERVES SIX TO EIGHT

MRS BEETON'S TIP

If you do not have a blender or food processor, rub the mango flesh through a sieve into a bowl and stir in the lime juice and sugar.

BLACKCURRANT MOUSSE

Fresh, frozen or canned fruit may be used,
with the amount of sugar adjusted according
to the sweetness of the fruit.

250 g / 9 oz fresh blackcurrants
50 g / 2 oz caster sugar
10 ml / 2 tsp lemon juice
10 ml / 2 tsp gelatine
125 ml / 4 fl oz double cream
2 egg whites
whipped cream to decorate

Reserve a few whole blackcurrants for decoration. Rub the rest through a sieve into a measuring jug, then make up the purée to 150 ml / ¼ pint with water.

Combine the blackcurrant purée, sugar and lemon juice in a mixing bowl. Place 30 ml / 2 tbsp water in a small heatproof bowl and sprinkle the gelatine on to the liquid. Set aside for 15 minutes until the gelatine is spongy. Stand the bowl over a saucepan of hot water and stir the gelatine until it has dissolved completely. Cool slightly.

Fold a little of the blackcurrant purée into the cooled gelatine, then whisk this mixture into the bowl of blackcurrant purée. Leave in a cool place until the mixture starts to set.

In a deep bowl, whip the cream until it just holds its shape, then fold into the blackcurrant mixture with a metal spoon. Whisk the egg whites in a clean,

FREEZER TIP
Frozen blackcurrant mousse
is delicious. Omit the gelatine
and freeze the mixture in ice trays.
Thaw for 15 minutes in the
refrigerator before serving.

grease-free bowl, and fold in. Make sure that the mixture is thoroughly and evenly blended but do not overmix.

Pour gently into a glass dish, a wetted 500-ml / 17-fl oz mould or individual glasses. Refrigerate for 1–2 hours until set, then turn out if necessary and decorate with whipped cream and the reserved blackcurrants.

SERVES FOUR

MARQUISE ALICE

oil for greasing
4 eggs or 1 whole egg and 2 yolks
75 g / 3 oz caster sugar
250 ml / 8 fl oz milk
few drops of vanilla essence
10 ml / 2 tsp gelatine
50 g / 2 oz praline (see Mrs Beeton's Tip), crushed
5–6 sponge fingers
60 ml / 4 tbsp kirsch
125 ml / 4 fl oz double cream
125 ml / 4 fl oz single cream

DECORATION
200 ml / 7 fl oz double cream, whipped
redcurrant jelly

Oil a 750-ml / 1¼-pint mould. Beat the eggs and sugar until fluffy and pale.

Warm the milk in a saucepan; do not let it boil. Slowly stir it into the egg mixture, then strain the custard into a heatproof bowl placed over hot water. Cook over very low heat until the custard thickens.

Strain the thickened custard into a bowl, stir in the vanilla essence and leave to one side until cool.

Place 60 ml / 4 tbsp water in a small bowl and sprinkle the gelatine on to the liquid. Set aside for 15 minutes until the gelatine is spongy. Stand the bowl over a saucepan of hot water and stir the gelatine until it has dissolved completely.

Add the praline and continue to stir until the sugar in the praline has similarly dissolved. Cool until tepid and add to the custard. Leave in a cool place until the mixture thickens at the edges, stirring from time to time.

Break the sponge fingers into small pieces and put into a mixing bowl. Add the kirsch and leave to soak. In a second bowl, combine the creams and whip until soft peaks form. Fold into the setting praline custard. Pour half the mixture into the mould and leave until thickened and beginning to set.

Arrange the soaked sponge fingers in an even layer all over the custard, leaving a 5 mm / ¼ inch clear border all around so that none of the sponge finger pieces will show when the pudding is turned out. Pour the rest of the mixture over the sponge finger pieces and refrigerate until set.

Turn out on to a wetted plate and decorate with lightly whipped cream. Warm the redcurrant jelly until it runs, then drizzle it over the cream. Serve at once.

SERVES FOUR TO SIX

MRS BEETON'S TIP

To make praline, heat 100 g / 4 oz sugar with 15 ml / 1 tbsp water until dissolved, then boil until golden. Stir in 100 g / 4 oz toasted blanched almonds and turn the mixture on to an oiled baking sheet to cool. Crush in a mortar with a pestle, or use a blender.

CHOCOLATE MARQUISE

150 g / 5 oz plain chocolate, coarsely grated
200 g / 7 oz unsalted butter, cubed
6 eggs, separated

Put the chocolate into a large heatproof bowl and place over hot water. Heat gently until the chocolate melts.

Gradually beat the butter into the chocolate, a cube at a time. Stir in the egg yolks, one by one. When all have been added and the mixture is smooth, remove the bowl from the heat.

In a clean, grease-free bowl, whisk the egg whites until stiff. Fold them into the chocolate mixture. Pour gently into a glass bowl or 6 individual dishes and chill thoroughly before serving.

SERVES SIX

MICROWAVE TIP
Melt the chocolate in a small bowl on High for 2½–3 minutes.

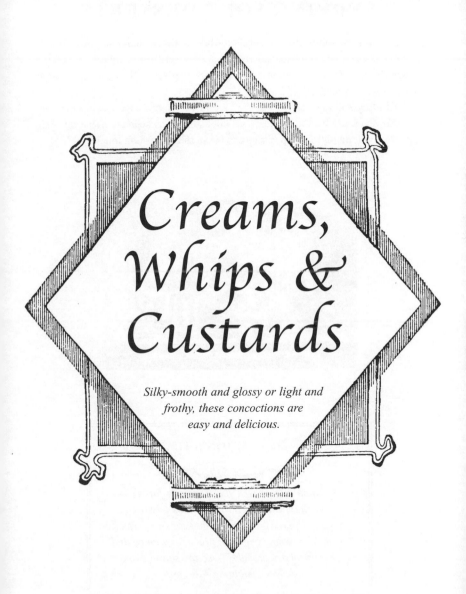

Creams, Whips & Custards

*Silky-smooth and glossy or light and
frothy, these concoctions are
easy and delicious.*

SERVING SOFT DESSERTS

Elegant glasses, dainty dishes and pretty bowls always make the best of soft creamy desserts. Swirl those desserts that are not set firm by lightly dragging a spoon through them. If you are short of dessert glasses, then substitute large wine glasses instead.

Chilling soft desserts so that they are just firm and nicely cold is important; however take care not to leave syllabubs that may separate in the refrigerator for too long. Offer crisp biscuits as the perfect finishing touch.

MRS BEETON'S TIP

Eggs should be chosen very carefully for recipes in which they are used raw. Always buy from a reputable source and ensure the eggs are perfectly fresh. Very young children, pregnant women and the infirm are probably best advised to avoid dishes containing raw eggs.

BANANA CUSTARD

500 ml / 17 fl oz milk
3 eggs plus 2 yolks
25 g / 1 oz caster sugar
few drops of vanilla essence
3 bananas (about 400 g / 14 oz)

DECORATION
30 ml / 2 tbsp crushed butterscotch or
grated chocolate or toasted flaked almonds

In a saucepan, bring the milk to just below boiling point. Put the eggs and sugar into a bowl, mix well, then stir in the scalded milk and vanilla essence. Strain the custard mixture into a heavy-bottomed saucepan or a heatproof bowl placed over a saucepan of simmering water. Alternatively, use a double saucepan, but make sure the water does not touch the upper pan.

Cook the custard over very gentle heat for 15–25 minutes, stirring all the time with a wooden spoon, until the custard thickens to the consistency of single cream. Stir well around the sides as well as the base of the pan or bowl to prevent the formation of lumps, especially if using a double saucepan. Do not let the custard boil or it may curdle.

As soon as the custard thickens, pour it into a jug to stop further cooking. Peel and slice the bananas and stir them into the custard. Stand the jug in a bowl of hot water for 5 minutes to allow the flavours to blend. Spoon into a serving dish or individual dishes and decorate with butterscotch, grated chocolate or flaked almonds.

If the custard is to be served cold, pour it into a bowl and cover the surface with a piece of dampened greaseproof paper to prevent discoloration and a skin forming. When cold, pour into a serving dish and decorate as desired.

SERVES FOUR

PINEAPPLE CUSTARD

1 x 376 g / 13 oz can crushed pineapple
25 g / 1 oz cornflour
400 ml / 14 fl oz milk
2 eggs, separated
25 g / 1 oz caster sugar

Drain the pineapple, pouring the juice into a jug and spreading the fruit out in an ovenproof dish. In a bowl, blend the cornflour to a smooth paste with a little of the milk. Heat the rest of the milk in a saucepan until it is just below boiling point, then pour on to the blended cornflour. Stir in well.

Return the mixture to the clean saucepan and bring to the boil, stirring all the time. Boil gently for 1–2 minutes. Remove from the heat and stir in the reserved pineapple juice.

Add the egg yolks to the cornflour sauce. Stir well. Return to the heat and cook very gently, without boiling, stirring all the time, until the mixture thickens. Remove from the heat and leave to cool; stir from time to time to prevent the formation of a skin. Set the oven at 140°C / 275°F / gas 1.

Pour the cooled custard over the crushed pineapple. In a clean, grease-free bowl, whisk the egg whites until stiff, then whisk in most of the sugar. Spread the meringue mixture over the custard, making sure that it is completely covered. Sprinkle with the remaining sugar. Bake for 30 minutes until the meringue is crisp and browned.

SERVES FOUR

BAKED CUSTARD

Egg dishes should be cooked by gentle heat.
If the custard is allowed to boil, the protein will no longer
be able to hold moisture in suspension and the
resultant pudding will be watery. It is therefore a wise
precaution to use a bain marie *or water bath.*

butter for greasing
500 ml / 17 fl oz milk
3 eggs
25 g / 1 oz caster sugar
grated nutmeg

Grease a baking dish. Set the oven at 140–150°C / 275–300°F / gas 1–2.

In a saucepan, bring the milk to just below boiling point. Put the eggs and sugar into a bowl, mix well, then stir in the scalded milk. Strain the custard mixture into the prepared dish. Sprinkle the nutmeg on top.

Stand the dish in a roasting tin and add enough hot water to come halfway up the sides of the dish. Bake for 1 hour or until the custard is set in the centre.

SERVES FOUR

PRESSURE COOKER TIP

Make the custard as described above, using a
dish that will fit inside your pressure cooker.
Pour 300–600 ml / ½–1 pint water into the cooker.
Stand the dish on a trivet in the cooker, close the lid
and bring to 15 lb pressure. Cook for 5 minutes.
Reduce the pressure slowly.

CRÈME BRÛLÉE

butter for greasing
15 ml / 1 tbsp cornflour
250 ml / 8 fl oz milk
250 ml / 8 fl oz single cream
few drops of vanilla essence
3 eggs
50 g / 2 oz caster sugar

Grease a 600-ml / 1-pint flameproof dish. In a bowl, blend the cornflour to a smooth paste with a little of the milk. Bring the rest of the milk to the boil in a saucepan.

Pour the boiling milk on to the blended cornflour, stirring well. Return the mixture to the clean pan, bring to the boil, and boil for 1 minute, stirring all the time. Remove from the heat and set the pan aside to cool.

Combine the cream, vanilla essence and eggs in a bowl and beat well. Stir into the cooled cornflour mixture. Whisk over low heat for about 30 minutes or until the custard thickens; do not boil. Add 25 g / 1 oz of the sugar and pour into the prepared dish. Sprinkle the pudding with the rest of the sugar.

Place under a preheated hot grill for 10 minutes or until the sugar has melted and turned brown. Keep the custard about 10 cm / 4 inches from the heat. Serve hot or cold.

SERVES FOUR

MRS BEETON'S TIP

The brûlée may be browned in a 200°C / 400°F / gas 6 oven if preferred. It will require about 15 minutes.

CRÈME BRÛLÉE
À LA GRANDE CATELET

An ideal dinner party dish. If serving cold, tap the caramel
crust sharply with the back of a spoon to break it up.

250 ml / 8 fl oz single cream or milk
250 ml / 8 fl oz double cream
1 vanilla pod or a few drops of vanilla essence or
15 ml / 1 tbsp brandy
6 egg yolks
about 75 g / 3 oz caster sugar

Put the cream or milk and the double cream in a double saucepan or a bowl over a saucepan of hot water. Add the vanilla pod, if used, and warm very gently. Meanwhile mix the egg yolks with 25 g / 1 oz of the caster sugar in a large bowl. Beat together thoroughly.

When the cream feels just warm to the finger, remove the pod, if used. Pour the cream on to the yolks, stir, and return to the double saucepan or bowl.

Continue to cook gently for about 40 minutes, stirring all the time with a wooden spoon, until the custard thickens to the consistency of single cream. When cooking the custard, scrape down the sides of the saucepan frequently with a spatula to prevent the formation of lumps and do not let the custard approach the boiling point. If a vanilla pod has not been used, add a few drops of vanilla essence or the brandy. Set the oven at 160°C / 325°F / gas 3.

Strain the custard into a shallow 600 ml / 1 pint flameproof dish, stand it on a baking sheet and bake for 5–10 minutes until a skin has formed on the top. Do not allow the custard to colour. Leave to cool, then refrigerate for at least 2–3 hours, or preferably overnight.

Heat the grill. Sprinkle enough of the remaining caster sugar over the surface of the custard to cover it entirely with an even, thin layer. Place the dish under the hot grill for 10–15 minutes or until the sugar melts and turns to caramel. Keep the top of the custard about 10 cm / 4 inches from the heat. Serve hot or cold.

SERVES FOUR

CARAMEL CUSTARD CUPS

100 g / 4 oz lump or granulated sugar
300 ml / ½ pint milk
100 ml / 3½ fl oz single cream
2 whole eggs and 2 yolks
25 g / 1 oz caster sugar
few drops of vanilla essence

Prepare four 150-ml / ¼-pint ovenproof moulds to receive a caramel coating (see Mrs Beeton's Tip).

Make the caramel by heating the lump sugar with 150 ml / ¼ pint water in a heavy-bottomed saucepan. Stir constantly until the sugar dissolves and the mixture comes to the boil. Continue to boil, without stirring, until the mixture is golden brown. Pour a little of the caramel on to a metal plate and set aside. Immediately pour the remaining caramel into the warmed moulds, twisting and turning each mould in turn until the sides and the base are evenly coated. Leave until cold and set. Set the oven at 140–150°C / 275–300°F / gas 1–2.

In a saucepan, bring the milk and cream to just below boiling point. Put the eggs and sugar into a bowl, mix well, then stir in the scalded milk. Add a few drops of vanilla essence. Strain the custard mixture into the prepared moulds.

Stand the moulds in a roasting tin and add hot water to come halfway up the sides of the moulds. Bake for 30 minutes or until the custard is set.

Remove the cooked custards and leave to stand for a few minutes, then invert each on an individual dessert plate. The caramel will run off and serve as a sauce. Break up the reserved caramel by tapping sharply with a metal spoon, and decorate the top of each custard with the pieces of broken caramel.

SERVES FOUR

MRS BEETON'S TIP

Hot caramel can cause nasty burns. The best way to safeguard yourself is by using a newspaper holder: prepare a thickly folded band of newspaper long enough to encircle the chosen mould. Heat the mould in boiling water or in the oven, then wrap the newspaper around it, twisting the ends tightly to form a handle. Make sure that the band is secure and the ends are tight enough to prevent slipping. Hold the paper, not the side of the mould, when tilting it to distribute the caramel and, as an additional safeguard, work over the sink.

ZABAGLIONE

4 egg yolks
40 g / 1½ oz caster sugar
60 ml / 4 tbsp Marsala or Madeira

Put the egg yolks into a deep heatproof bowl and whisk lightly. Add the sugar and wine, and place the bowl over a saucepan of hot water. Whisk for about 10 minutes or until the mixture is very thick and creamy (when the whisk is lifted, the trail should lie on top of the miture for 2–3 seconds).

Pour the custard into individual glasses and serve while still warm, accompanied by sponge fingers.

SERVES FOUR

VARIATION

• **Zabaglione Cream** Dissolve 50 g / 2 oz caster sugar in 60 ml / 4 tbsp water in a saucepan and boil for 1–2 minutes until syrupy. Whisk with the egg yolks until pale and thick. Add 30 ml / 2 tbsp Marsala or Madeira and 30 ml / 2 tbsp single cream while whisking. The finely grated rind of ½ lemon can be added, if liked. Spoon into individual glasses and chill before serving.

MRS BEETON'S TRIFLE

Plain whisked or creamed sponge cake, individual buns,
or Madeira cake are ideal for this trifle. Originally, Mrs Beeton
made her custard by using 8 eggs to thicken 600 ml / 1 pint milk,
cooking it slowly over hot water. Using cornflour and egg yolks is
more practical and it gives a creamier, less 'eggy' result.

4 slices of plain cake or individual cakes
6 almond macaroons
12 ratafias
175 ml / 6 fl oz sherry
30–45 ml / 2–3 tbsp brandy
60–90 ml / 4–6 tbsp raspberry or strawberry jam
grated rind of 1 lemon
25 g / 1 oz flaked almonds
300 ml / ½ pint double cream
30 ml / 2 tbsp icing sugar
candied and crystallized fruit and peel to decorate

CUSTARD
25 g / 1 oz cornflour
25 g / 1 oz caster sugar
4 egg yolks
5 ml / 1 tsp vanilla essence
600 ml / 1 pint milk

Place the sponge cakes in a glass dish. Add the macaroons and ratafias, pressing them down gently. Pour about 50 ml / 2 fl oz of the sherry into a basin and set it aside, then pour the rest over the biscuits and cake. Sprinkle with the brandy. Warm the jam in a small saucepan, then pour it evenly over the trifle base, spreading it lightly. Top with the lemon rind and almonds.

For the custard, blend the cornflour, caster sugar, egg yolks and vanilla to a smooth cream with a little of the milk. Heat the remaining milk until hot. Pour some of the milk on the egg mixture, stirring, then replace the mixture in the saucepan with the rest of the milk. Bring to the boil, stirring constantly, and simmer for 3 minutes.

Pour the custard over the trifle base and cover the surface with a piece of dampened greaseproof paper. Set aside to cool.

Add the cream and icing sugar to the reserved sherry and whip until the mixture stands in soft peaks. Swirl the cream over the top of the trifle and chill. Decorate with pieces of candied and crystallized fruit and peel before serving.

SERVES SIX

FRENCH CHOCOLATE CREAMS

This is incredibly rich, so a little goes a long way.

150 ml / ¼ pint milk
60 ml / 4 tbsp caster sugar
pinch of salt
100 g / 4 oz plain chocolate, coarsely grated
100 g / 4 oz unsalted butter, in small pieces
8 egg yolks

Warm the milk, sugar and salt in a small saucepan and stir until the sugar dissolves. Set the pan aside.

Combine the chocolate and butter in a large heatproof bowl and place over hot water. Heat gently, stirring constantly, until the mixture is quite smooth and all the solids have melted.

Add the milk to the chocolate mixture, stirring it in thoroughly. Using a balloon whisk if possible, beat in the egg yolks one at a time. On no account allow the mixture to curdle.

Divide the cream between 6 small pots or ramekins. Chill well before serving.

SERVES SIX

DEAN'S CREAM

*This is a very old recipe for a dessert that was one
of the forerunners of the standard modern trifle.*

6 individual sponge cakes
raspberry jam
apricot jam
100 g / 4 oz ratafias
250 ml / 8 fl oz sherry
75 ml / 5 tbsp brandy
500 ml / 17 fl oz double cream
50 g / 2 oz caster sugar

DECORATION
angelica
glace cherries
crystallized pineapple

Cut the sponge cakes in half lengthways, and spread half with raspberry jam and half with apricot jam. Arrange them in a deep glass dish, jam sides facing upwards.

Break the ratafias into pieces and sprinkle on top of the sponge cakes. Pour the sherry over the cakes and leave to soak for about 30 minutes.

Put the brandy, cream, and sugar into a bowl and whisk until very thick. Pile into the dish and decorate with angelica, cherries and crystallized pineapple. Chill well before serving.

SERVES EIGHT

SWISS CREAM

100 g / 4 oz ratafias, sponge fingers or
sponge cake
60 ml / 4 tbsp sweet sherry
35 g / 1¼ oz arrowroot
500 ml / 17 fl oz milk
1.25 ml / ¼ tsp vanilla essence
pinch of salt
30–45 ml / 2–3 tbsp caster sugar
grated rind and juice of 1 lemon
150 ml / ¼ pint double cream

DECORATION
10 ml / 2 tsp flaked almonds
4 glacé cherries, halved

Break the biscuits or cake into small pieces and place on the base of a glass dish or individual dishes. Pour over the sherry.

Put the arrowroot in a bowl and mix to a paste with a little of the milk. Mix the remaining milk with the vanilla essence and salt in a heavy-bottomed saucepan. Bring to the boil, then pour on to the blended paste, stirring briskly to prevent the formation of lumps.

Return the mixture to the clean pan and heat until it thickens and boils, stirring all the time. Stir in the caster sugar until dissolved. Remove the pan from the heat, cover the surface of the mixture with greased greaseproof paper to prevent the formation of a skin, and set aside until cold.

Stir the lemon rind and juice into the cold arrowroot mixture. In a bowl, whip the cream until soft peaks form, then stir lightly into the pudding mixture. Pour over the soaked biscuits or cake and refrigerate for about 2 hours to set. Decorate with almonds and cherries.

SERVES FOUR TO SIX

QUICK JELLY CREAM

1 x 127 g / 4½ oz tablet orange jelly
45 ml / 3 tbsp orange juice
30 ml / 2 tbsp custard powder
250 ml / 8 fl oz milk
125 ml / 4 fl oz double cream

Chop the jelly tablet roughly. Heat 100 ml / 3½ fl oz water in a saucepan, add the jelly, and stir until dissolved. Add the orange juice and leave to cool.

Meanwhile, in a bowl, blend the custard powder with a little of the milk. Put the rest of the milk into a saucepan and bring to the boil. Pour the hot milk slowly on to the blended custard powder, stirring all the time. Return to the clean pan, bring to the boil and boil for 1–2 minutes, stirring continuously, until the custard thickens.

Cool the custard slightly, then stir into the jelly. Cool until beginning to set.

In a bowl, whip the cream until it leaves a trail, then fold into the setting mixture. Pour into 4 individual glasses and chill for about 1 hour. Decorate as desired.

SERVES FOUR

VARIATIONS

- **Pineapple Jelly Cream** Use a pineapple jelly tablet and the juice from a 376 g / 13 oz can of crushed pineapple. Fold the fruit into the setting mixture.
- **Berry Jelly Cream** Use a raspberry or strawberry jelly tablet and the juice from a 219 g / 7½ oz can of raspberries or strawberries. Fold the fruit into the setting mixture.

DAMASK CREAM

600 ml / 1 pint single cream
1 blade of mace
10-cm / 4-inch piece of cinnamon stick
20 ml / 4 tsp icing sugar, sifted
triple-strength rose-water
15 ml / 1 tbsp rennet essence (vegetarian rennet
is available in healthfood shops)

DECORATION
deep pink rose petals or 1 red rose

Pour 500 ml / 17 fl oz of the cream into a saucepan, add the mace and cinnamon stick, and heat almost to boiling point. Remove from the heat and infuse for 20–30 minutes.

Strain the cream into a clean bowl, discarding the spices. Add 10 ml / 2 tsp icing sugar to the cream with rose-water to taste. Cool to blood-heat and stir in the rennet. Pour gently into a decorative 750-ml / 1¼-pint serving bowl and leave to set in a warm room until cold and firm.

Pour the remaining cream into a jug. Flavour with rose-water and very gently pour the flavoured cream over the set cream to a depth of 5 mm / ¼ inch. Sprinkle lightly all over with the remaining icing sugar.

Strew deep-pink rose petals around the edge of the dish or set one perfect red rosebud in the centre. Serve with thin, crisp, plain or almond biscuits.

SERVES FOUR

VELVET CREAM

*This basic recipe produces one of the simplest and most
delicious of desserts, the full cream. It lends itself to
a wide range of variations and may be served in glasses
or as a decorative mould (see Mrs Beeton's Tip).*

**10 ml / 2 tsp gelatine
50 g / 2 oz caster sugar
30 ml / 2 tbsp sherry or a few drops of vanilla essence
250 ml / 8 fl oz double cream
250 ml / 8 fl oz single cream**

Place 45 ml / 3 tbsp water in a small bowl and sprinkle the gelatine on to the
liquid. Set aside for 15 minutes until the gelatine is spongy. Stand the bowl over
a saucepan of hot water and stir the gelatine until it has dissolved completely.
Add the sugar and sherry or vanilla essence and continue to stir until the sugar
has dissolved. Set aside.

Combine the creams in a mixing bowl and whip lightly. Fold the flavoured gelatine mixture into the cream and divide between 4 glasses or individual dishes.
Refrigerate for 1–2 hours or until set. When the cream has set, a thin top layer
of fresh fruit jelly may be added, if liked.

SERVES FOUR

VARIATIONS

In each of the variations below, omit the sherry or vanilla essence.

- **Almond Cream** Flavour with 1.25 ml / ¼ tsp almond essence. Decorate with
  browned almonds.
- **Berry Cream** Use 375 ml / 13 fl oz double cream and fold in 125 ml / 4 fl oz
  raspberry or strawberry purée instead of single cream. Decorate with fresh
  berry fruits.
- **Chocolate Cream** Flavour with 75 g / 3 oz melted plain chocolate. Decorate
  the top with chocolate curls.

- **Coffee Cream** Flavour with 15 ml / 1 tbsp instant coffee dissolved in 15 ml / 1 tbsp boiling water and cooled. Add 15 ml / 1 tbsp rum, if liked, and decorate with coffee beans.
- **Highland Cream** Flavour with 15 ml / 1 tbsp whisky and serve with a whisky-spiked apricot sauce.
- **Lemon and Almond Cream** Flavour with 30 ml / 2 tbsp lemon juice, 5 ml / 1 tsp grated lemon rind and 25 g / 1 oz ground almonds.
- **Liqueur Cream** Flavour with 15 ml / 1 tbsp Tia Maria, curaçao, kirsch or Advocaat.
- **Pistachio Cream** Blanch, skin and finely chop 100 g / 4 oz pistachio nuts and fold into the mixture before adding the gelatine. Tint the cream pale green with food colouring.

MRS BEETON'S TIP

The cream may be made in a mould, if preferred.
Make up one quantity of Fresh Lemon Jelly (page 2).
Use some of the jelly to line a 750-ml / 1 ¼-pint
mould, decorating it with cut shapes of angelica
and glacé cherry. When the jelly lining has set,
carefully add the prepared cream and refrigerate
for 2–3 hours until set. The remaining jelly
may be set in a shallow tray, then chopped
for use as a decoration.

VANILLA BAVAROIS

*A bavarois, or Bavarian Cream, as it is sometimes known,
consists of a cup custard combined with cream and
flavouring, with gelatine as the setting agent.*

**oil for greasing
4 egg yolks or 1 whole egg and 2 yolks
50 g / 2 oz caster sugar
250 ml / 8 fl oz milk
2.5 ml / ½ tsp vanilla essence
10 ml / 2 tsp gelatine
150 ml / ¼ pint double cream
150 ml / ¼ pint single cream**

Oil a 750-ml / 1¼-pint mould. In a bowl, beat the eggs and sugar together until fluffy and pale.

Warm the milk in a saucepan; do not let it boil. Slowly stir it into the egg mixture, then strain the custard back into the clean pan or into a double saucepan or heatproof bowl placed over hot water. Cook over very low heat until the custard thickens.

Strain the thickened custard into a bowl, stir in the vanilla essence and set aside until cool.

Place 15 ml / 1 tbsp water in a small bowl and sprinkle the gelatine on to the liquid. Set aside for 15 minutes until the gelatine is spongy. Stand the bowl over a saucepan of hot water and stir the gelatine until it has dissolved completely. Allow to cool until tepid and add to the custard. Leave in a cool place until the mixture thickens at the edges, stirring from time to time to prevent the formation of a skin.

Combine the creams in a bowl and whip lightly. Fold into the custard mixture, and pour into the prepared mould. Refrigerate for about 2 hours until set, then turn out on to a flat wetted plate to serve.

SERVES FOUR TO SIX

VARIATIONS

- **Caramel Bavarois** Dissolve 100 g / 4 oz granulated sugar in 15 ml / 1 tbsp water. Heat until the syrup turns a rich brown colour. Carefully stir in 60 ml / 4 tbsp hot water, remove from the heat, and stir until all the caramel dissolves. Stir into the warm custard.
- **Chocolate Bavarois** Grate 100 g / 4 oz plain chocolate and add with the milk. It will melt in the warm custard. Add 5 ml / 1 tsp vanilla essence.
- **Coffee Bavarois** Dissolve 15 ml / 1 tbsp instant coffee in 15 ml / 1 tbsp boiling water. Cool, then stir in 15 ml / 1 tbsp rum. Add this essence with the milk.
- **Crème Diplomate** Soak 100 g / 4 oz chopped crystallized fruit in 30 ml / 2 tbsp kirsch. Pour the vanilla Bavarian cream into the mould to a depth of 1.5 cm / ¾ inch and leave to set. Spread half the fruit over it and cover with a little of the cream. Leave to set. Continue alternating layers of fruit and cream, finishing with a layer of cream. Allow each layer to set before adding the next.
- **Crème Tricolore** Divide the mixture into three portions. Flavour the first with vanilla essence, the second with chocolate, the third with strawberry purée. Line the mould with vanilla cream in the same way as when lining with jelly (see Mrs Beeton's Tip, page 91). When this is completely set, fill alternately with equal layers of the chocolate and strawberry creams, allowing each layer to set before adding the next.
- **Ribbon Bavarois** Divide the mixture into two portions, and flavour and colour each half separately; for example, with vanilla and chocolate, vanilla and orange, or ginger and chocolate. Do not decorate the mould but oil it lightly. Pour in one of the creams to a depth of 1.5 cm / ¾ inch, leave to set, then repeat with the second cream. Continue in this way until all the mixture is used.

MRS BEETON'S DUTCH FLUMMERY

This is best made the day before it is to be served.

25 g / 1 oz gelatine
grated rind and juice of 1 lemon
4 eggs, beaten
500 ml / 17 fl oz dry sherry
50 g / 2 oz caster sugar

Place 125 ml / 4 fl oz water in a small bowl and sprinkle the gelatine on to the liquid. Set aside for 15 minutes until the gelatine is spongy. Stand the bowl over a saucepan of hot water and stir the gelatine until it has dissolved completely. Pour the mixture into a measuring jug and make up to 500 ml / 17 fl oz with cold water. Add the grated lemon rind and strain in the juice.

In a second bowl, beat the eggs, sherry and sugar together. Add to the gelatine mixture. Pour into the top of a double saucepan, place over simmering water and cook over low heat, stirring all the time, until the mixture coats the back of the spoon. Do not let the mixture boil.

Strain the mixture into a wetted 1.75-litre / 3-pint mould and refrigerate until set. Turn out on to a plate to serve.

SERVES FOUR TO SIX

MRS BEETON'S TIP

It is often difficult to centre a moulded dessert on a serving plate. Wet the plate first, shaking off excess moisture. When the dessert is inverted on to the plate, the thin skin of liquid on the plate will make it easy to move it into the desired position.

MRS BEETON'S CHARLOTTE RUSSE

45 ml / 3 tbsp icing sugar, sifted
24 sponge fingers
15 ml / 1 tbsp gelatine
500 ml / 17 fl oz single cream
45 ml / 3 tbsp any sweet liqueur
1 x 15 cm / 6 inch round sponge cake,
1 cm / ½ inch thick

In a small bowl, mix 30 ml / 2 tbsp of the icing sugar with a little water to make a thin glacé icing. Cut 4 sponge fingers in half and dip the rounded ends in the icing. Line a 15-cm / 6-inch soufflé dish with the halved fingers, placing them like a star, with the sugared sides uppermost and the iced ends meeting in the centre. Dip one end of each of the remaining biscuits in the icing; use to line the sides of the dish, with the sugared sides outward and the iced ends at the base. Trim the biscuits to the height of the soufflé dish.

Place 45 ml / 3 tbsp water in a small heatproof bowl and sprinkle the gelatine on to the liquid. Set aside for 15 minutes until the gelatine is spongy. Stand the bowl over a saucepan of hot water and stir the gelatine until it has dissolved completely.

Combine the cream, liqueur and remaining icing sugar in a bowl. Add the gelatine and whisk until frothy. Stand the mixture in a cool place until it begins to thicken, then pour carefully into the charlotte. Cover the flavoured cream with the sponge cake, making sure it is set enough to support the cake. Chill for 8–12 hours, until firm.

Loosen the biscuits from the sides of the dish with a knife, carefully turn the charlotte out on to a plate and serve.

SERVES SIX

PINEAPPLE BUTTERMILK WHIP

This is a very good dessert for slimmers.

**400 ml / 14 fl oz unsweetened pineapple or
orange juice
15 ml / 1 tbsp gelatine
150 ml / ¼ pint buttermilk**

Place 60 ml / 4 tbsp of the fruit juice in a small bowl and sprinkle the gelatine on to the liquid. Set aside for 15 minutes until the gelatine is spongy. Stand the bowl over a saucepan of hot water and stir the gelatine continuously until it has dissolved completely.

Combine the gelatine mixture with the remaining fruit juice. Pour a little of the mixture into each of 4 stemmed glasses.

Chill the rest of the juice mixture for about 1 hour. When it is on the point of setting, whisk in the buttermilk until frothy. Spoon into the glasses and chill.

SERVES FOUR

MRS BEETON'S TIP

*Take care, when adding the creamy
mixture to the glasses, not to
disturb the jelly layer.*

LEMON FLUFF

30 ml / 2 tbsp lemon juice
30 ml / 2 tbsp cornflour
75 ml / 5 tbsp caster sugar
5 ml / 1 tsp grated lemon rind
2 eggs, separated
125 ml / 4 fl oz single cream

In a bowl, blend the lemon juice with the cornflour. Bring 150 ml / ¼ pint water to the boil in a saucepan. Stir a little of the boiling water into the cornflour mixture, then add the contents of the bowl to the remaining boiling water. Bring the mixture back to the boil, stirring constantly, then boil for 1–2 minutes until the mixture thickens. Stir in 45 ml / 3 tbsp of the caster sugar with the lemon rind. Remove the pan from the heat.

Add the egg yolks to the lemon mixture, stirring them in vigorously. Cover the mixture with dampened greaseproof paper to prevent the formation of a skin, and cool until tepid.

Stir the cream into the cooled lemon custard. In a clean, grease-free bowl, whisk the egg whites until stiff, add the remaining sugar and whisk until stiff again. Fold the egg whites into the lemon mixture until evenly distributed. Spoon into 4 glasses and chill before serving.

SERVES FOUR

MRS BEETON'S TIP

*When grating the lemon, be sure
to remove only the outer rind and
not the bitter pith.*

CIDER SYLLABUB

A syllabub was originally a sweet, frothy drink made with cider or mead mixed with milk straight from the cow. Mrs Beeton's original syllabub recipe combined 600 ml / 1 pint of sherry or white wine with 900 ml / 1½ pints of fresh, frothy milk. Nutmeg or cinnamon and sugar was stirred in, and clotted cream may have been added. When cider was used instead of wine, brandy was added to enrich the syllabub. It is now a rich creamy dessert, often made light and frothy by the addition of egg whites.

grated rind and juice of ½ lemon
50 g / 2 oz caster sugar
125 ml / 4 fl oz sweet cider
15 ml / 1 tbsp brandy
250 ml / 8 fl oz double cream

In a large bowl, mix the lemon rind and juice with the caster sugar, cider and brandy. Stir until the sugar is dissolved.

Put the cream in a mixing bowl. Whip until it stands in stiff peaks. Gradually fold in the lemon and cider mixture. Pour the mixture into stemmed glasses and refrigerate for about 2 hours. Remove 20 minutes before serving to allow the flavours to 'ripen'.

SERVES FOUR

WINE SYLLABUB

This syllabub has a frothy head, with the lemon juice and wine settling in the bottom of the glasses.

200 ml / 7 fl oz double cream
2 egg whites
75 g / 3 oz caster sugar
juice of ½ lemon
100 ml / 3½ fl oz sweet white wine or sherry
crystallized lemon slices to decorate

In a large bowl, whip the cream until it just holds its shape. Put the egg whites in a clean, grease-free mixing bowl and whisk until they form soft peaks. Fold the sugar into the egg whites, then gradually add the lemon juice and wine or sherry.

Fold the egg white mixture into the whipped cream. Pour into glasses and refrigerate for about 2 hours. Remove 20 minutes before serving. Serve decorated with the crystallized lemon slices.

SERVES FOUR

WHIPPED SYLLABUB

50 ml / 2 fl oz sweet red wine or ruby port
250 ml / 8 fl oz double cream
50 ml / 2 fl oz medium dry sherry
juice of ½ orange
grated rind of ½ lemon
50 g / 2 oz caster sugar

Divide the wine or port between 4 chilled stemmed glasses, and keep chilled. In a bowl, whip the cream, adding the remaining ingredients gradually, in order, until the mixture just holds firm peaks.

Pile the cream mixture into the chilled glasses (see Mrs Beeton's Tip). Serve as soon as possible.

SERVES FOUR

MRS BEETON'S TIP

When adding the cream mixture to the chilled
wine take care not to mix the two. The wine should
clearly be seen in the bottom of each glass.

CRANACHAN

125 g / 4½ oz coarse oatmeal
400 ml / 14 fl oz double cream
50 g / 2 oz caster sugar
15 ml / 1 tbsp rum
150 g / 5 oz fresh raspberries

Toast the oatmeal under a low grill until lightly browned (see Mrs Beeton's Tip). Set aside to cool.

In a bowl, whip the cream until stiff. Stir in the toasted oatmeal and flavour with the sugar and rum.

Hull the raspberries. Stir them into the cream or layer with the Cranachan mixture, reserving 4 perfect fruit for decoration, if liked. Serve in 4 individual glass dishes.

SERVES FOUR

MRS BEETON'S TIP

When toasting the oatmeal, shake the grill pan frequently so that the mixture browns evenly.

Cheesecakes
& Cream Pies

*Sunday treats or lavishly decorated dinner-party
desserts, zesty cheesecakes and creamy
chiffon pies are guaranteed to
satisfy your guests.*

The cheesecakes that are popular today tend to be American-style concoctions, with gelatine as the setting agent. However, the traditional cuisines of European countries offer alternative recipes for baked cheesecakes that are zesty with lemon and fruity with sultanas, delicate and creamy with Italian ricotta cheese, or more substantial in the tradition of British baking.

For uncooked recipes made with soft cheese, the cheese used may be varied according to individual requirements. Use cream cheese for a rich result or lighter curd cheese (or sieved cottage cheese) for a cheesecake with a lower fat content. Plain yogurt or fromage frais may be used instead of cream in some recipes.

Recipes for baked cheesecakes should be followed more closely as the type of cheese used may well affect the result and yogurt or fromage frais may separate out during cooking.

A CHOICE OF BASE

Which base, or case, to use to hold the cheese mixture depends on the type of cheesecake being made. Cooked cheesecakes may be set in a sweet pastry case or on a base of pastry; alternatively a sponge cake mixture may form the base. Uncooked cheesecakes are usually set in a case or on a base made of biscuit crumbs and butter.

BISCUIT BASE

Quick and easy to make, a biscuit base is ideal for uncooked cheesecakes. Although a biscuit base can be used for cooked cheesecakes, the biscuits tend to become slightly overcooked and the fat which binds them seeps out during cooking.

To line the base only of a 20-cm / 8-inch container you will need about 100 g / 4 oz crushed biscuits combined with 50 g / 2 oz butter. Digestive biscuits or other plain sweet biscuits are usually used; however chocolate-coated biscuits, gingernuts or coconut cookies may be crushed to vary the flavour of the base.

Crush the biscuits in a food processor if you have one. Otherwise, place them in a strong polythene bag and use a rolling pin to crush them. It is best to close the bag loosely with a metal tie to allow air to escape. Crush the biscuits carefully to avoid breaking the bag and making a mess.

Melt the butter in a saucepan, then stir in the crushed biscuits off the heat. Alternatively, melt the butter in a mug or small bowl in the microwave, allowing about 1 minute on High, then pour it over the biscuits in a dish. Stir well.

When the mixture is pressed on to the base of the container, smooth it over with the back of a clean metal spoon. Allow the base to cool, then chill it before adding the topping.

To line the sides of the container as well as the base, double the quantity of biscuits and butter and turn all the mixture into the container. Use a metal spoon to press the mixture all over the base and up the sides. This is only practical for a shallow container, such as a flan dish or tin.

PASTRY CASE

A case of sweet pastry is often used for a baked cheesecake. The ingredients and method are included in the relevant recipes. To vary the pastry slightly, spices, a few finely chopped or ground nuts (almonds or hazelnuts), grated lemon or orange rind may be added.

CAKE BASE

This type of base is used for cooked cheesecakes. A one-stage mixture of fat, egg and flour may be used and spread in the container before the topping is added.

A cake base may be made for an uncooked cheesecake. Set the oven at 180°C / 350°F / gas 4. In a mixing bowl, beat together 50 g / 2 oz each of butter, caster sugar and self-raising flour with 1 egg and 5 ml / 1 tsp baking powder. When all the ingredients are thoroughly combined, spread the mixture in a well-greased 20-cm / 8-inch sandwich tin and bake for 20–25 minutes, until risen and golden. The cake should feel firm on top when cooked. Turn it out on to a wire rack to cool.

Trim the top of the cake level before placing it in the base of a 20 cm / 8 inch deep cake tin. Set the cheesecake mixture on top. For a very thin base to a shallow cheesecake, slice through the cake horizontally and use one half. Pack and freeze the second slice for making a second cheesecake. The base may be frozen for up to 3 months.

TURNING OUT A CHEESECAKE

To remove a cheesecake from a loose-bottomed flan tin, have ready a storage jar or small soufflé dish. Make sure that the jar has a flat, heat-resistant lid if the cheesecake is fresh from the oven. Stand the tin containing the cheesecake on top of the jar, so that the loose base is well supported and the side is free. Gently ease the side away from the cheesecake, then transfer the dessert on its base to a flat platter.

FREEZING CHEESECAKES

Baked and fairly firm uncooked cheesecakes freeze very well. Freeze the whole cheesecake before adding any decoration. A cheesecake which is decorated with piped cream should be open frozen, then put in a large, deep, rigid container and returned to the freezer.

Any leftover cheesecake may be frozen in slices. Arrange the slices in a rigid container or on a double thickness of foil, placing a piece of freezer film between each slice. Close the foil loosely around the slices or cover the container and place in a level place in the freezer.

A decorated cheesecake may be frozen successfully for 2–3 weeks ready to be served for a special dessert. Slices of cheesecake may be frozen for up to 2 or 3 months. They will not look their best but will taste good as an impromptu family pudding.

ALMOND CHEESECAKE

butter for greasing
75 g / 3 oz curd cheese
50 g / 2 oz butter, melted
2 eggs, separated
grated rind and juice of ½ lemon
50 g / 2 oz ground almonds
50 g / 2 oz caster sugar
30 ml / 2 tbsp self-raising flour

Line and grease a 15-cm / 6-inch sandwich cake tin. Set the oven at 220°C / 425°F / gas 7.

Rub the curd cheese through a sieve into a mixing bowl. Add the melted butter, egg yolks, lemon rind and juice, almonds and caster sugar and mix thoroughly. Sift the flour over the mixture and fold in.

In a clean, grease-free bowl, whisk the egg whites until stiff. Fold into the almond mixture. Spoon the mixture into the prepared tin and bake for 10 minutes.

Lower the oven temperature to 180°C / 350°F / gas 4 and cook for about 15 minutes more. Test to see whether the cake is cooked (see Mrs Beeton's Tip). If necessary, return the cake to the oven for a few minutes, covering the surface loosely with foil or greaseproof paper to prevent overbrowning.

SERVES FOUR

MRS BEETON'S TIP

To test the cake, insert a thin heated skewer into the centre. If the skewer comes out dry, the cake is cooked.

LEMON CHEESECAKE

BASE
100 g / 4 oz digestive biscuits
50 g / 2 oz butter
25 g / 1 oz caster sugar

FILLING
200 g / 7 oz full-fat soft cheese
75 g / 3 oz caster sugar
2 eggs, separated
125 ml / 4 fl oz soured cream
15 g / ½ oz gelatine
grated rind and juice of 1 lemon

Make the base. Crumb the biscuits (see page 102). Melt the butter in a small saucepan and mix in the crumbs and sugar. Press the mixture on to the base of a loose-bottomed 15-cm / 6-inch cake tin. Put in a cool place to set.

Make the filling. In a mixing bowl, beat the cheese and sugar together. Add the egg yolks and beat well. Stir in the soured cream.

Place 45 ml / 3 tbsp water in a small bowl. Sprinkle the gelatine on to the liquid. Set aside for 15 minutes until the gelatine is spongy. Stand the bowl over a pan of hot water and stir the gelatine until it has dissolved completely. Stir the lemon rind, juice and dissolved gelatine into the cheese mixture.

In a clean, grease-free bowl, whisk the egg whites until stiff and fold carefully into the mixture. Pour into the prepared tin and chill for 45–60 minutes until firm. When quite cold, remove from the tin, transfer to a plate and slice to serve.

SERVES FOUR TO SIX

CLASSIC BAKED CHEESECAKE

BASE
75 g / 3 oz butter
150 g / 5 oz fine white breadcrumbs, dried
50 g / 2 oz caster sugar
7.5 ml / 1½ tsp ground cinnamon

FILLING
3 eggs, separated
100 g / 4 oz caster sugar
375 g / 13 oz full-fat soft cheese
grated rind and juice of 1 lemon
125 ml / 4 fl oz soured cream
icing sugar for dusting

Set the oven at 180°C / 350°F / gas 4. Make the base. Melt the butter in a frying pan and stir in the breadcrumbs. Cook over gentle heat, stirring until the crumbs are golden. Remove from the heat; stir in the sugar and cinnamon. Press the crumbs over the base of a loose-bottomed 18-cm / 7-inch cake tin.

Beat the egg yolks in a mixing bowl until liquid. Add the sugar to the egg yolks, beating until creamy. Rub the cheese through a sieve into the bowl, then work in lightly. Add the lemon rind and juice to the mixture with the soured cream.

In a clean, grease-free bowl, whisk the egg whites to soft peaks. Stir 30 ml / 2 tbsp into the cheese mixture, then fold in the rest lightly. Turn the mixture gently on to the prepared base in the tin. Bake for 45 minutes. Cover loosely with foil and bake for a further 15 minutes. Cool in the tin. Serve dusted with icing sugar.

SERVES TEN

CHEDDAR CHEESECAKE

BASE
175 g / 6 oz plain flour
75 g / 3 oz margarine
1 egg yolk
flour for rolling out

FILLING
1 egg, separated, plus 1 white
grated rind and juice of 1 lemon
75 ml / 5 tbsp plain yogurt
25 g / 1 oz self-raising flour
75 g / 3 oz caster sugar
150 g / 5 oz Cheddar cheese, grated

Set the oven at 200°C / 400°F / gas 6. To make the pastry base, sift the flour into a bowl, then rub in the margarine until the mixture resembles fine bread-crumbs. Add the egg yolk and just enough water (about 15–30 ml / 1–2 tbsp) to mix the ingredients into a short pastry. Press the pastry together gently with your fingertips.

Roll out the pastry on a lightly floured surface and use to line a 20-cm / 8-inch flan ring or dish. Bake 'blind' (see Mrs Beeton's Tip). Lower the oven temperature to 160°C / 325°F / gas 3.

In a mixing bowl, combine the egg yolk, lemon rind and juice, yogurt, flour and sugar. Mix well, then fold in the grated cheese.

In a clean, grease-free bowl, whisk both egg whites until stiff. Stir 15 ml / 1 tbsp of the beaten egg whites into the cheese mixture to lighten it, then gently fold in the remaining egg white. Turn into the prepared pastry case.

Bake in the preheated oven for 35–45 minutes or until firm in the centre and lightly browned. Serve cold.

SERVES SIX TO EIGHT

MRS BEETON'S TIP

To bake blind, prick the base of the pastry case with a fork, then cover with a piece of greaseproof paper. Fill the pastry case with dried beans, bread crusts or rice and bake at 200°C / 400°F / gas 6 for 10 minutes. Remove the paper and beans or other dry filling and return the case to the oven for 5 minutes to dry out the inside before adding the chosen filling and returning the case to the oven. If a fully cooked pastry case is required, as when a cold filling is to be added, bake the pastry case blind for 20–30 minutes, and dry out for 5–7 minutes.

VARIATIONS

- **Cheshire Cheesecake** Substitute Cheshire cheese for the Cheddar. Either grate it finely or crumble the Cheshire cheese, then crush it with a fork until it breaks down into fine crumbs. Cheshire is milder and slightly more tangy than Cheddar.
- **Apple and Cheddar Cheesecake** Spread a layer of stewed apples or sweetened apple purée in the pastry case before adding the cheese filling.
- **Glacé Fruit Cheesecake** Sprinkle a mixture of glacé and candied fruit and peel over the pastry case before adding the cheese mixture. Chopped angelica, cherries, candied peel and crystallized ginger are suitable.
- **Individual Cheesecakes** Make individual cheesecakes in patty tins.

APPLE CHEESECAKE

This is not a cheesecake in the modern sense,
but a tart filled with apple cheese (or apple curd).
It is refreshing and delicious.

350 g / 12 oz puff pastry, thawed if frozen
450 g / 1 lb cooking apples, peeled,
cored and sliced
100 g / 4 oz caster sugar
100 g / 4 oz butter, melted
grated rind and juice of 1 lemon
2 eggs plus 2 egg yolks

Set the oven at 200°C / 400°F / gas 6. Roll out the pastry and use to line a 25-cm / 10-inch flan dish or tin. Prick the pastry all over, then chill for 20 minutes in the bottom of the refrigerator or 10 minutes in the freezer. Bake for 20 minutes. Remove the pastry case from the oven. Reduce the oven temperature to 180°C / 350°F / gas 4.

Place the apples in a saucepan and add 30 ml / 2 tbsp water. Cook over medium heat, stirring, until the fruit begins to soften. Allow to simmer gently and cover the pan. Stir occasionally until the apples are reduced to a pulp, then press them through a sieve into a bowl.

Stir the sugar, butter and lemon rind and juice into the apples. Beat the eggs and yolks together, then strain them through a fine sieve into the apple mixture. Beat well and pour the mixture into the pastry case. Bake for 25–30 minutes, until the apple filling is set.

Leave to cool, then serve with fresh cream or fromage frais.

SERVES TWELVE

MELOPITA

*In Greece, this honey-flavoured dessert would be made
from myzithra, a soft cheese made from ewe's milk.
Sieved cottage cheese is an acceptable substitute.*

BASE
300 g / 11 oz plain flour
7.5 ml / 1½ tsp baking powder
pinch of salt
125 g / 4½ oz butter
flour for rolling out

FILLING
675 g / 1½ lb cottage cheese
150 g / 5 oz caster sugar
10 ml / 2 tsp ground cinnamon
200 g / 7 oz clear honey
5 eggs

Set the oven at 180°C / 350°F / gas 4. To make the pastry base, sift the flour, baking powder and salt into a bowl, then rub in the butter until the mixture resembles fine breadcrumbs. Add enough cold water to mix the ingredients to a stiff pastry.

Roll out the pastry on a lightly floured surface and use to line a 25-cm / 10-inch flan tin or dish. Line with greaseproof paper and sprinkle with baking beans or dried peas. Bake for 20 minutes; remove paper and beans or peas.

Rub the cottage cheese through a sieve into a mixing bowl and add the sugar, half the cinnamon, and the honey. Mix lightly, then add the eggs, one at a time, beating well after each addition. Rub the mixture through a sieve into a clean bowl, then turn into the pastry shell.

Bake for 45 minutes, then leave to cool in the oven. Serve cold, sprinkled with the remaining cinnamon.

SERVES TEN TO TWELVE

TORTA DI RICOTTA

BASE
100 g / 4 oz butter or margarine
75 g / 3 oz icing sugar
2 egg yolks
pinch of ground cinnamon
250 g / 9 oz plain flour
flour for rolling out

FILLING
675 g / 1½ lb ricotta cheese
25 g / 1 oz grated Parmesan cheese
2 eggs
25 g / 1 oz plain flour
45 ml / 3 tbsp plain yogurt
50 g / 2 oz caster sugar
grated rind and juice of 1 lemon
pinch of salt
few drops of lemon essence

DECORATION AND SAUCE
225 g / 8 oz fresh raspberries
15 ml / 1 tbsp arrowroot
100 g / 4 oz raspberry jam
60 ml / 4 tbsp maraschino liqueur
125 ml / 4 fl oz sweet red vermouth

Make the pastry. Cream the butter or margarine with the sugar in a mixing bowl until light and fluffy. Blend in the egg yolks, cinnamon and flour. Knead the mixture lightly and roll into a ball. Chill for 20 minutes.

Set the oven at 200°C / 400°F / gas 6. Roll out the pastry on a lightly floured surface to line a 25-cm / 10-inch flan ring set on a baking sheet (see Mrs Beeton's Tip). Prick the base with a fork and chill for 30 minutes. Line with greaseproof paper and sprinkle with baking beans or dried peas. Bake for 20 minutes; remove paper and beans or peas. Lower the oven temperature to 180°C / 350°F / gas 4.

For the filling, rub the ricotta through a sieve, then beat it with the Parmesan in a bowl and gradually beat in the rest of the filling ingredients. Spoon into the partially cooked flan case, level the surface and bake for about 50 minutes. Cover loosely with foil if the top becomes too dark. The filling should be firmly set when cooked. Leave to cool in the tin.

Decorate the cooled flan with the raspberries, and chill while making the sauce. Put the arrowroot in a small bowl and mix to a thin cream with 125 ml / 4 fl oz water. Melt the jam in a saucepan. When it boils, stir in the arrowroot mixture to thicken it. Flavour with the maraschino liqueur and vermouth. Remove from the heat and when cold, pour a little of the sauce over the raspberries. Serve the rest separately.

SERVES EIGHT

MRS BEETON'S TIP

To line the flan ring, place on the baking sheet and roll the pastry to a round at least 5 cm / 2 inches larger than the ring. The pastry should be about 3 mm / ⅛ inch thick. Lift the pastry round over a rolling pin to prevent it breaking and stretching, and lay it in the flan ring. Press the pastry gently down on the baking sheet and into the base of the ring. Working from the centre outwards, press the pastry into the base and up the sides, making sure it fits snugly into the flutes, if present, and is of even thickness all round. Trim off any surplus pastry by rolling across the top of the ring with the rolling pin.

PEPPERMINT CREAM PIE

Decorate this delectable pie with crushed peppermint crisp chocolate for a party or other special occasion.

PIE SHELL
100 g / 4 oz gingernut biscuits
50 g / 2 oz plain chocolate
50 g / 2 oz butter

FILLING
2 egg yolks
75 g / 3 oz caster sugar
few drops of peppermint essence
10 ml / 2 tsp gelatine
125 ml / 4 fl oz double cream

Make the pie shell. Place the biscuits between two sheets of greaseproof paper (or in a stout polythene bag) and crush finely with a rolling pin. Alternatively, crumb in a food processor.

Melt the chocolate and butter in a heatproof bowl over gently simmering water. Stir in the crumbs thoroughly. Press the mixture in an even layer all over the base and sides of a shallow 18-cm / 7-inch pie plate. Put in a cool place until the shell has set.

MRS BEETON'S TIP

Peppermint essence is very strong, so use sparingly. The best way to do this is to dip a cocktail stick or thin wooden skewer into the essence, then add just one drop at a time to the mixture.

Make the filling. Combine the egg yolks and sugar in a heatproof bowl. Stir in 45 ml / 3 tbsp cold water and stand the bowl over a saucepan of simmering water. Whisk the mixture until thick and pale, then whisk in the peppermint essence (see Mrs Beeton's Tip).

Place 30 ml / 2 tbsp water in a small bowl, and sprinkle the gelatine on to the liquid. Set aside for 15 minutes until the gelatine is spongy. Stand the bowl over a pan of hot water and stir the gelatine until it has dissolved completely. Cool for 5 minutes, then whisk into the peppermint mixture.

In a bowl, whisk the cream lightly. Fold it into the peppermint mixture, then turn into the chocolate crumb shell and refrigerate for about 1 hour until set.

SERVES FOUR

COCONUT CREAM PIE

PIE SHELL
100 g / 4 oz digestive biscuits
50 g / 2 oz butter
25 g / 1 oz sugar

FILLING
40 g / 1½ oz cornflour
pinch of salt
40 g / 1½ oz caster sugar
300 ml / ½ pint milk
1 egg yolk
25 g / 1 oz butter
few drops of vanilla essence
75 g / 3 oz desiccated coconut

Make the pie shell. Place the biscuits between two sheets of greaseproof paper (or in a stout polythene bag) and crush finely with a rolling pin. Alternatively, crumb in a food processor.

Melt the butter in a small saucepan and mix in the crumbs and sugar. Press the mixture in an even layer all over the base and sides of a shallow 18-cm / 7-inch pie plate. Put in a cool place until the shell has set.

Make the filling. Put the cornflour, salt and sugar in a bowl and stir in enough of the milk to make a smooth cream. Bring the rest of the milk to the boil in a saucepan. Pour it on to the cornflour mixture, stirring constantly, then return the mixture to the pan.

Bring the filling to the boil again, stirring constantly. Cook, still stirring virgorously, for 1–2 minutes, until the sauce thickens. Beat in the egg yolk, butter, vanilla essence and coconut.

Cool the filling until tepid, then spoon into the pie shell. When cold, refrigerate for 1–2 hours before serving.

SERVES FOUR

COFFEE CHIFFON PIE

PIE SHELL
75 g / 3 oz digestive biscuits
50 g / 2 oz butter
25 g / 1 oz walnuts, chopped
25 g / 1 oz sugar

FILLING
100 g / 4 oz caster sugar
10 ml / 2 tsp gelatine
15 ml / 1 tbsp instant coffee
2 eggs, separated
pinch of salt
10 ml / 2 tsp lemon juice
whipped cream to decorate

Make the pie shell. Place the biscuits between two sheets of greaseproof paper (or in a stout polythene bag) and crush finely with a rolling pin. Alternatively, crumb in a food processor. Melt the butter in a small saucepan and mix in the crumbs, chopped nuts and sugar. Press the mixture in an even layer over the base and sides of a shallow 18-cm / 7-inch pie plate. Put in a cool place to set.

To make the filling, mix 50 g / 2 oz of the sugar with the gelatine in a cup. Put the coffee into a measuring jug, add 45 ml / 3 tbsp boiling water, and stir until dissolved. Make up the liquid with cold water to 250 ml / 8 fl oz. Pour the coffee liquid into a heatproof bowl or the top of a double saucepan. Add the egg yolks, mix well, then place over gently simmering water. Stir in the gelatine mixture, with a pinch of salt. Cook over gentle heat for about 15 minutes, stirring constantly until the custard thickens slightly. Do not let the mixture boil. Pour into a cold bowl, cover with dampened greaseproof paper and chill until on the point of setting, then stir in the lemon juice.

In a clean, grease-free bowl, whisk the egg whites until foamy. Gradually whisk in the remaining sugar and continue whisking until stiff and glossy. Fold the coffee custard into the meringue, pour into the pie shell and chill for at least 1 hour until set. Serve decorated with whipped cream.

SERVES FOUR

LEMON CHIFFON PIE

PIE SHELL
100 g / 4 oz digestive biscuits
50 g / 2 oz butter
25 g / 1 oz sugar

FILLING
100 g / 4 oz caster sugar
10 ml / 2 tsp gelatine
3 eggs, separated
grated rind and juice of 2 lemons

Make the pie shell. Place the biscuits between two sheets of greaseproof paper (or in a stout polythene bag) and crush finely with a rolling pin. Alternatively, crumb the biscuits in a food processor.

Melt the butter in a small saucepan and mix in the crumbs and sugar. Press the mixture in an even layer all over the base and sides of a shallow 18-cm / 7-inch pie plate. Put in a cool place until the shell has set.

To make the filling, mix 50 g / 2 oz of the caster sugar with the gelatine in a small bowl. Combine the egg yolks, lemon juice and 50 ml / 2 fl oz water in a heatproof bowl or the top of a double saucepan. Mix lightly, then stir in the gelatine mixture.

Cook over gently simmering water for 10 minutes, stirring all the time, until the custard thickens. Do not let it boil. Pour into a cold bowl, cover with dampened greaseproof paper and chill until on the point of setting. Stir in the lemon rind.

In a clean, grease-free bowl, whisk the egg whites until foamy. Gradually whisk in the remaining sugar and continue to whisk until stiff and glossy. Fold the lemon custard mixture into the meringue, pile into the pie shell and chill for at least 1 hour until set.

SERVES FOUR

VARIATIONS

- **Chocolate Orange Chiffon Pie** Make the pie shell using plain chocolate digestive biscuits. Follow the instructions for Orange Chiffon Pie (below).
- **Lime Chiffon Pie** Make the pie shell. For the filling substitute 3 limes for the lemons. If the limes are very small and not over juicy, add an additional 30 ml / 2 tbsp lemon juice.
- **Orange Chiffon Pie** Make the pie shell. For the filling, substitute oranges for the lemons, but use the grated rind of a single fruit. Add 15 ml / 1 tbsp lemon juice to the orange juice and enough water to make the liquid up to 150 ml / ¼ pint. Use this with the egg yolks, gelatine and 15 ml / 1 tbsp sugar, to make a custard. When whisking the egg whites, add only 40 g / 1½ oz sugar.

COEUR À LA CRÈME
AU CITRON

150 ml / ¼ pint double cream
pinch of salt
150 g / 5 oz low-fat curd cheese
50 g / 2 oz caster sugar
grated rind and juice of 1 lemon
2 egg whites

Line a 400-ml / 14-fl oz heart-shaped coeur à la crème mould with greaseproof paper. In a bowl whip the cream with the salt until it holds soft peaks. Break up the curd cheese with a fork, and whisk it gradually into the cream with the sugar. Do not let the mixture lose stiffness.

Fold the lemon rind and juice into the cream as lightly as possible.

In a clean, grease-free bowl, whisk the egg whites until they hold stiff peaks. Fold them into the mixture, then very gently turn the mixture into the mould, filling all the corners.

Stand the mould in a large dish or roasting tin to catch the liquid which seeps from the mixture. Chill for at least 2 hours or overnight. Turn out and serve with single cream.

SERVES SIX

MRS BEETON'S TIP

Individual coeur à la crème moulds
may be used. If these are
unavailable, clean yogurt pots,
with several drainage holes punched
in the base of each, make an
acceptable substitute.

Rice & Milk Puddings

The ultimate in comfort food, ranging from inexpensive weekday puddings to more sophisticated set milk puddings.

PRESSURE COOKING

Milk puddings may be cooked in a pressure cooker. This gives good, creamy results in a fraction of the time needed for baking or simmering. Do not use less than 600 ml / 1 pint of milk and keep the heat at a steady temperature which is low enough to prevent the milk from rising too high in the cooker and blocking the vent. For the same reason the cooker should not be more than a quarter full when cooking a milk pudding.

MICROWAVE COOKING

The microwave oven may be used to cook milk puddings. However, puddings using rice, tapioca, macaroni or semolina boil over very readily. For this reason a medium or low microwave power setting should be used and the pudding should be cooked in a very large dish – a mixing bowl covered with a suitable dinner plate or very deep casserole is ideal. The advantage of cooking milk puddings thickened with rice in the microwave is a matter of personal opinion. Since a low power setting has to be used the time saving is not enormous and this cooking method demands attention to ensure that the pudding does not boil over. As an alternative to traditional recipes, the following is an excellent microwave method for making an extravagant, deliciously creamy rice pudding.

Put 50 g / 2 oz short-grain rice in a covered dish. Add 600 ml / 1 pint water and cook on High for 20–25 minutes. At the end of the cooking time all the water should have been absorbed and the grains of rice should be swollen and sticky. Immediately stir in sugar to taste and 300 ml / ½ pint double or single cream. The pudding may be dotted with butter and sprinkled with a little grated nutmeg, then lightly browned under a moderate grill.

RICE PUDDING

This basic recipe works equally well with flaked rice,
sago or flaked tapioca.

butter for greasing
100 g / 4 oz pudding rice
1 litre / 1¾ pints milk
pinch of salt
50–75 g / 2–3 oz caster sugar
15 g / ½ oz butter (optional)
1.25 ml / ¼ tsp grated nutmeg

Butter a 1.75-litre / 3-pint pie dish. Wash the rice in cold water, drain and put it into the dish with the milk. Leave to stand for 30 minutes.

Set the oven at 150°C / 300°F / gas 2. Stir the salt and sugar into the milk mixture and sprinkle with flakes of butter, if used, and nutmeg.

Bake for 2–2¼ hours or until the pudding is thick and creamy, and brown on the top. The pudding is better if it cooks even more slowly, at 120° / 250°F / gas ½ for 4–5 hours.

SERVES FOUR TO FIVE

PRESSURE COOKER TIP

Bring all the ingredients to the boil
in the open cooker, stirring. Reduce
the heat so that the milk just bubbles.
Put the lid on and bring to
15 lb pressure without increasing
the heat. Cook for 12 minutes.
Reduce pressure slowly.

SWEDISH RICE

300 g / 11 oz long-grain rice
pinch of salt
625 g / 1¼ lb cooking apples
pared rind of 1 lemon
375 ml / 13 fl oz milk
75 g / 3 oz caster sugar
1.25 ml / ¼ tsp ground cinnamon
100 ml / 3½ fl oz sweet sherry
100 g / 4 oz raisins
single cream to serve

Wash the rice, drain it and put it in a saucepan. Add boiling salted water to cover and cook for 3 minutes; drain well.

Peel and core the apples and slice them thinly into a second pan. Add the rice, lemon rind and milk and simmer gently for about 45 minutes until tender. Remove the rind.

Stir the sugar, cinnamon, sherry, and raisins into the mixture and cook for a further 4–5 minutes. Spoon into individual bowls and serve with cream.

SERVES SIX

ICED RICE PUDDING

*Serve cooled poached fruit, such as plums, apricots or pears,
or a fruit salad with this frozen dessert.*

**1 litre / 1¾ pints milk
175 g / 6 oz pudding rice
225 g / 8 oz sugar
6 egg yolks
5 ml / 1 tsp vanilla essence**

Pour the milk into a heavy-bottomed saucepan, then stir in the rice and sugar. Bring to the boil, stirring occasionally to make sure the sugar dissolves and the rice does not stick, then lower the heat and cover the pan. Cook gently for 2 hours, stirring occasionally, or until the rice is thick and creamy. Remove from the heat and beat well.

Lightly whisk the egg yolks, then strain them through a fine sieve into the hot rice and beat well. Stir in the vanilla, then pour the rice into a mould, cake tin or container for freezing.

Cover the surface of the rice with dampened greaseproof paper and leave until cold. Freeze until firm, preferably overnight.

Leave the rice in a cool room or on a high shelf in the refrigerator for about 40 minutes before turning it out on to a serving platter.

SERVES EIGHT

PEAR AND RICE MERINGUE

butter for greasing
75 g / 3 oz long-grain rice
750 ml / 1¼ pints milk
pinch of salt
1 bay leaf
40 g / 1¼ oz granulated sugar
25 g / 1 oz butter
2 eggs, separated
6 fresh or canned pear halves
50 g / 2 oz caster sugar
caster sugar for dredging

Butter a 1.5-litre / 2½-pint pie dish. Wash the rice, drain and place in a heavy-bottomed saucepan with the milk, salt and bay leaf. Simmer for about 1 hour, until the rice is tender. Remove the bay leaf.

Set the oven at 140°C / 275°F / gas 1. Stir the granulated sugar and butter into the rice mixture. Cool slightly, then add the egg yolks, mixing well. Pour into the prepared pie dish. Arrange the pear halves, cut side down, on top.

In a clean, grease-free bowl, whisk the egg whites until stiff and fold in the caster sugar in spoonfuls. Pile on top of the rice and pears. Dredge the meringue with a little caster sugar and bake for about 20 minutes or until the meringue is crisp and golden brown. Serve immediately.

SERVES SIX

MRS BEETON'S TIP

*Bay leaves are a valuable addition to the
store cupboard or freezer. Although primarily
used in stews, stocks and fish dishes, they
add a subtle flavour to milk puddings.*

EMPRESS PUDDING

butter for greasing
100 g / 4 oz long-grain rice
1 litre / 1¾ pints milk
pinch of salt
50 g / 2 oz butter or margarine
50 g / 2 oz caster sugar
200 g / 7 oz jam or stewed fruit

SHORT CRUST PASTRY
75 g / 3 oz plain flour
pinch of salt
40 g / 1½ oz margarine (or half butter, half lard)
flour for rolling out

Butter the base of a 1.25-litre / 2-pint ovenproof dish. Make the pastry. Sift the flour and salt into a bowl, then rub in the margarine until the mixture resembles fine breadcrumbs. Add enough cold water to make a stiff dough. Press the dough together with your fingertips. Set the pastry aside in a cool place while preparing the rice filling.

Wash the rice, drain and place in a heavy-bottomed saucepan. Add the milk and salt and simmer for about 1 hour or until tender. Stir in the butter or margarine and sugar.

Set the oven at 180°C / 350°F / gas 4. Roll out the pastry on a lightly floured surface and line the sides of the baking dish. Spread a layer of the rice mixture on the base of the dish and cover with jam or fruit. Repeat the layers until the dish is full, finishing with a layer of rice. Bake for 25–30 minutes. Serve with Apricot Sauce (page 228).

SERVES SIX

WINDSOR PUDDING

butter for greasing
40 g / 1½ oz long-grain rice
350 ml / 12 fl oz milk
450 g / 1 lb cooking apples
grated rind of ½ lemon
50 g / 2 oz caster sugar
3 egg whites

Butter a 1-litre / 1¾-pint pudding basin or soufflé dish. Wash the rice, drain thoroughly and place in a saucepan with the milk. Simmer for 45–60 minutes or until the rice is tender and all the milk has been absorbed. Cool slightly.

Peel, core and roughly chop the apples. Stew in a heavy-bottomed covered saucepan until soft. Shake the pan from time to time to prevent the apples from sticking. Prepare a steamer or half fill a large saucepan with water. Bring to the boil.

Purée the apples with the lemon rind in a blender or food processor. Alternatively, rub the apples through a sieve into a bowl, in which case add the grated lemon rind afterwards. Stir in the cooked rice and sugar.

In a clean, grease-free bowl, whisk the egg whites until fairly stiff and stir them into the apple mixture. Spoon the mixture into the prepared pudding basin or soufflé dish, cover with greased greaseproof paper or foil and secure with string.

Put the pudding in the perforated part of the steamer, or stand it on an old saucer or plate in the pan of boiling water. The water should come halfway up the sides of the basin. Cover the pan tightly and steam the pudding over gently simmering water for 45 minutes. Serve the pudding hot.

SERVES SIX

MRS BEETON'S TIP

Windsor pudding is very light and it can be difficult to turn out. Placing a small circle of non-stick baking parchment in the bottom of the basin helps. Alternatively, serve the pudding straight from the basin or dish.

GENEVA PUDDING

butter for greasing
75 g / 3 oz long-grain rice
750 ml / 1¼ pints milk
pinch of salt
75 g / 3 oz caster sugar
1 kg / 2¼ lb cooking apples
50 g / 2 oz butter
1.25 ml / ¼ tsp ground cinnamon

Butter a 1.5-litre / 2½-pint pie dish. Wash the rice and put it into a saucepan with the milk. Add the salt and simmer for about 1 hour or until the rice grains are tender. Set the oven at 180°C / 350°F / gas 4.

Stir 25 g / 1 oz of the sugar into the rice mixture. Set aside.

Peel, core, and chop the apples. Put them into a second saucepan along with the butter and cinnamon. Add 45 ml / 3 tbsp water. Simmer gently until soft, then purée in a blender or food processor or push through a sieve. Stir in the remaining sugar.

Arrange the rice and apple in alternate layers in the pie dish, with rice on the top and bottom. Bake for 20–30 minutes.

SERVES SIX

CHILLED RICE MOULD

150 g / 5 oz pudding rice
1 litre / 1¾ pints milk
75 g / 3 oz sugar
vanilla essence
25 g / 1 oz butter

Wash the rice in cold water, drain and place in the top of a double saucepan with the milk. Cover the pan and cook the mixture gently over simmering water for 2–2½ hours until the grain is tender and the milk almost absorbed. Stir occasionally to prevent the grain from settling on the bottom of the pan.

Stir the sugar, vanilla essence to taste and the butter into the mixture and pour into a wetted 1-litre / 1¾-pint mould or basin. Chill until set. Turn out and serve with stewed fruit or jam.

SERVES FOUR TO SIX

CHOCOLATE SEMOLINA

800 ml / 27 fl oz milk
65 g / 2½ oz semolina
75 g / 3 oz plain chocolate
50 g / 2 oz caster sugar
few drops of vanilla essence

Heat 750 ml / 1¼ pints of the milk in a heavy-bottomed saucepan. Sprinkle in the semolina, stir well, and simmer for 15–20 minutes or until the semolina is cooked.

Meanwhile, grate the chocolate into a second pan, add the remaining milk and heat until the chocolate has melted. Stir into the semolina with the sugar and essence, and serve at once.

SERVES FOUR TO FIVE

SEMOLINA PUDDING

Use coarsely ground rice, oatmeal, small sago or
cornmeal instead of semolina, if preferred.

1 litre / 1¾ pints milk
flavouring (see Mrs Beeton's Tip)
75 g / 3 oz semolina
pinch of salt
50–75 g / 2–3 oz caster sugar
butter for greasing (optional)

Warm the milk in a heavy-bottomed saucepan. Add any solid flavouring, if used, to the milk and infuse for about 10 minutes; then remove.

Sprinkle the semolina on to the milk, stirring quickly to prevent the formation of lumps. Bring to simmering point, stirring all the time. Continue stirring, and simmer for 15–20 minutes or until the grain is transparent and cooked through.

Stir in the salt, sugar, and any flavouring essence used. Serve the creamed semolina hot or cold or pour into a well-buttered 1.75-litre / 3-pint pie dish, and bake at 180°C / 350°F / gas 4 for 20–30 minutes until the top has browned.

SERVES SIX

MRS BEETON'S TIP

Grated citrus rind, ground cinnamon,
allspice or grated nutmeg may
be added to all these puddings.
Flavouring essences or liqueurs are
equally suitable. A pinch of salt
improves the flavour of all puddings.

HONEY PUDDING

butter for greasing
125 ml / 4 fl oz milk
25 g / 1 oz semolina
2 eggs, separated
25 g / 1 oz butter
100 g / 4 oz honey
grated rind of ½ lemon
2.5 ml / ½ tsp ground ginger
150 g / 5 oz dried white breadcrumbs

Butter a 600–750-ml / 1–1¼-pint pudding basin. Prepare a steamer or half fill a large saucepan with water and bring to the boil.

Heat the milk in a heavy-bottomed saucepan. Sprinkle in the semolina and cook for 10 minutes, stirring all the time.

Remove the pan from the heat and add the egg yolks, butter, honey, lemon rind, ginger and breadcrumbs. Beat well.

In a clean, grease-free bowl, whisk the egg whites until fairly stiff. Fold into the semolina mixture. Pour the mixture into the prepared basin, cover with greased greaseproof paper or foil and secure with string.

Put the pudding in the perforated part of the steamer, or stand it on an old saucer or plate in the pan of boiling water. The water should come halfway up the sides of the basin. Cover the pan tightly and steam the pudding over gently simmering water for 1¾–2 hours.

Serve from the basin or leave for 5–10 minutes at room temperature to firm up, then turn out on to a serving plate. Serve with Almond Sauce (page 217).

SERVES FIVE TO SIX

TAPIOCA CREAM PUDDING

butter for greasing
75 g / 3 oz tapioca
750 ml / 1¼ pints milk
pinch of salt
15 g / ½ oz butter or margarine
15 ml / 1 tbsp caster sugar
1.25 ml / ¼ tsp almond essence
3 eggs, separated
75 g / 3 oz ratafias or small macaroons, crushed

Butter a 1.1-litre / 2-pint pie dish. Wash the tapioca, drain and place in a saucepan with the milk and salt. Soak for 1–2 hours.

Heat the tapioca mixture and simmer for about 1 hour until the grain is soft and all the milk has been absorbed. Set the oven at 180°C / 350°F / gas 4.

Remove the tapioca mixture from the heat and stir in the butter, sugar and essence. Cool slightly, then stir in the egg yolks. Pour the mixture into the prepared pie dish and bake for 15–30 minutes.

Lower the oven temperature to 140°C / 275°F / gas 1. In a clean, grease-free bowl, whisk the egg whites until stiff. Fold in the crushed ratafias or macaroons. Pile the meringue topping on top of the tapioca mixture, return to the oven and bake for 20–30 minutes until the topping is crisp and golden brown. Serve at once.

SERVES SIX

OATMEAL FLUMMERY

150 g / 5 oz fine oatmeal
juice of 1 orange
15 ml / 1 tbsp caster sugar or honey

Put the oatmeal in a large bowl. Add 500 ml / 16 fl oz water and soak for 24 hours.

Transfer the oatmeal mixture to a large measuring jug. Measure an equal volume of water. Place the oatmeal mixture and measured water in a large bowl, and soak for a further 24 hours.

Strain the mixture through a fine sieve into a heavy-bottomed saucepan, squeezing or pressing the oatmeal to extract as much of the floury liquid as possible. Add the orange juice and sugar or honey.

Stir over gentle heat for 15–30 minutes or until the mixture boils and is very thick. Serve warm.

SERVES FOUR TO SIX

AMERICAN INDIAN PUDDING

butter for greasing
750 ml / 1¼ pints milk
75 g / 3 oz white or yellow cornmeal
100 g / 4 oz caster sugar
1.25 ml / ¼ tsp ground cinnamon or nutmeg
25 g / 1 oz butter
maple syrup to serve

Grease a 1 litre / 1¾ pint pie dish. Set the oven at 140–150°C / 275–300°F / gas 1–2. Bring the milk to the boil in a heavy-bottomed saucepan, then pour in the cornmeal. Cook over gentle heat for 5 minutes, stirring continuously, until thickened.

Remove the pan from the heat and stir in the sugar, spice and butter. Pour into the prepared pic dish. Bake the pudding for 1 hour until browned on top. Serve with maple syrup.

SERVES FOUR

CORNMEAL PUDDING

butter for greasing
500 ml / 17 fl oz milk
75 g / 3 oz white or yellow cornmeal
75 g / 3 oz caster sugar
50 g / 2 oz seedless raisins
grated rind and juice of ½ lemon
2 eggs, beaten

Grease a 900-ml / 1¾-pint pie dish. Set the oven at 180°C / 350°F / gas 4. Bring the milk to just below boiling point in a heavy-bottomed saucepan. Pour in the cornmeal. Cook over gentle heat for 5 minutes, stirring all the time, until the mixture thickens. Remove from the heat and stir in the sugar and raisins with the lemon rind and juice. Cool slightly.

Add the beaten eggs to the mixture, transfer to the prepared pie dish and level the top. Bake for 50–60 minutes until risen and browned on top. Scrve with cream or ice cream.

SERVES FOUR

BLANCMANGE

*Blancmange may be made using ground rice or arrowroot
instead of the cornflour given below. The quantities will be the same.
Traditionally, blancmange was a white mould which was flavoured
with sweet and bitter almonds. Use natural almond essence
to give this mould the best flavour.*

**75 g / 3 oz cornflour
1 litre / 1¾ pints milk
50 g / 2 oz sugar
a little almond essence**

In a bowl, blend the cornflour to a smooth paste with a little of the cold milk. Bring the remaining milk to the boil in a saucepan.

Pour the boiling milk on to the cornflour mixture, stirring all the time. Pour the mixture back into the pan and heat gently, stirring all the time until the mixture simmers and thickens. Allow to simmer for 5–10 minutes, stirring occasionally.

Remove the pan from the heat and stir in the sugar. Add almond essence to taste, stir well, then pour the blancmange into a wetted 1.1-litre / 2-pint mould. Press dampened greaseproof paper or microwave cooking film on to the surface of the blancmange and cool.

Chill the cooled blancmange for at least 2 hours, or until set. Unmould the blancmange just before serving.

SERVES SIX

FLAVOURINGS

- To keep the mould a creamy colour, vanilla, grated lemon rind or a good knob of butter with 125 ml / 4 fl oz sherry may be added instead of the almond essence. However, the mixture may also be flavoured with ingredients that add colour although the result is not strictly a blancmange.

- **Chocolate** Either add 30 ml / 2 tbsp cocoa to the cornflour and mix it to a paste or add 175 g / 6 oz plain chocolate, broken into squares, to the cooked mixture. Stir the mixture until the chocolate has melted before pouring it into the wetted mould.
- **Coffee** Dissolve 15 ml / 1 tbsp instant coffee in 15 ml / 1 tbsp boiling water, then stir in 30 ml / 2 tbsp rum. Stir this essence into the cooked mixture before pouring it into the mould.
- **Strawberry** Substitute 300 ml / ½ pint fresh strawberry purée for the same volume of milk, adding it to the cornflour mixture before stirring in the boiling milk.

MRS BEETON'S TIP

If arrowroot is used instead of cornflour, the pan should be removed from the heat as soon as the mixture has reached a full boil. If arrowroot is cooked for any length of time after boiling, it tends to thin down.

ARROWROOT PUDDING

The method below is suitable for all powdered grains,
including cornflour, custard powder, finely ground
rice or fine oatmeal.

1 litre / 1¾ pints milk
flavouring (see Blancmange, page 136)
65 g / 2½ oz arrowroot
pinch of salt
50–75 g / 2–3 oz caster sugar
butter for greasing (optional)

Warm the milk in a heavy-bottomed saucepan. Add any solid flavouring, if used, to the milk and infuse for 30 minutes; then remove.

Put the arrowroot in a bowl and blend with a little of the milk. In a saucepan bring the remaining milk to boiling point with the salt, and pour on to the blended paste, stirring briskly to prevent the formation of lumps.

Return the mixture to the clean pan, heat until it thickens, and simmer for 2–3 minutes to cook the grain completely, stirring all the time. Add the sugar and any liquid flavouring used.

Serve the arrowroot pudding as it is, hot or cold, or pour into a well-buttered 1.75-litre / 3-pint pie dish, and bake for 20–30 minutes at 180°C / 350°F / gas 4 until the top has browned.

SERVES SIX

Batter Puddings

Different types of batter are used to create several styles of sweet course, from much-loved pancakes to hearty baked puddings and crisp, light fritters.

EVERYDAY PANCAKES

*Pancakes are much too good to be reserved
exclusively for Shrove Tuesday. Simple, versatile,
and always popular, they lend themselves
to a wide range of savoury and sweet fillings.*

**100 g / 4 oz plain flour
1.25 ml / ¼ tsp salt
1 egg, beaten
250 ml / 8 fl oz milk, or half milk and half water
oil for frying**

Make the batter. Sift the flour and salt into a bowl, make a well in the centre and add the beaten egg. Stir in half the milk (or all the milk, if using a mixture of milk and water), gradually working the flour down from the sides.

Beat vigorously until the mixture is smooth and bubbly, then stir in the rest of the milk (or the water), Pour into a jug. The mixture may be left to stand at this stage, in which case it should be covered and stored in the refrigerator.

Heat a little oil in a clean 18-cm / 7-inch pancake pan. Pour off any excess oil, leaving the pan covered with a thin film of grease. Stir the batter and pour about 30–45 ml / 2–3 tbsp into the pan. There should be just enough to thinly cover the base. Tilt and rotate the pan so that the batter runs over the surface evenly.

Cook over moderate heat for about 1 minute until the pancake is set and golden brown underneath. Make sure the pancake is loose by shaking the pan, then either toss it or turn it with a palette knife or fish slice. Cook the second side for about 30 seconds or until golden.

Slide the pancake out on to a warmed plate. Serve at once, with a suitable filling or sauce, or keep warm over simmering water while making 7 more pancakes in the same way. Add more oil to the pan when necessary.

MAKES EIGHT

VARIATIONS

- **Rich Pancakes** Add 15 g / ½ oz cooled melted butter or 15 ml / 1 tbsp oil to the batter with 1 egg yolk. Alternatively, enrich the batter by adding 1 whole egg.
- **Cream Pancakes** Use 150 ml / ¼ pint milk and 50 ml / 2 fl oz single cream instead of 250 ml / 8 fl oz milk. Add 2 eggs and 25 g / 1 oz cooled melted butter, then stir in 15 ml / 1 tbsp brandy with caster sugar to taste. The mixture should only just coat the back of a spoon as the pancakes should be very thin.

SWEET PANCAKE FILLINGS

- **Apple** In a bowl, mix together 250 ml / 8 fl oz sweetened thick apple purée, 50 g / 2 oz sultanas and a pinch of cinnamon.
- **Apricot** Add 15 ml / 1 tbsp cinnamon to the batter when making the pancakes. For the filling, soak 50 g / 2 oz dried apricots in 60 ml / 4 tbsp water in a saucepan, then simmer with 50 g / 2 oz sugar and a generous squeeze of lemon juice until they are soft and pulpy. Add 25 g / 1 oz chopped toasted almonds.
- **Banana** In a bowl, mash 4 bananas with 50 g / 2 oz softened butter, 30 ml / 2 tbsp sugar and the grated rind and juice of 1 lemon.
- **Chocolate and Whipped Cream** Whip 150 ml / ¼ pint double cream with 15–30 ml / 1–2 tbsp icing sugar until it stands in soft peaks. Gently fold in 100 g / 4 oz grated chocolate and 30 ml / 2 tbsp finely chopped toasted hazelnuts. Swirl this on the pancakes, fold into quarters and serve at once.
- **Curd Cheese** In a bowl, beat 100 g / 4 oz curd cheese with 45 ml / 3 tbsp double cream, 30 ml / 2 tbsp caster sugar and the grated rind of ½ lemon. Add 40 g / 1½ oz sultanas.
- **Dried Fruit** Put 100 g / 4 oz chopped raisins, dates and cut mixed peel into a small saucepan with 100 ml / 3½ fl oz apple juice. Simmer until syrupy.
- **Ginger and Banana** Add 15 ml /1 tbsp ground ginger to the batter when making the pancakes, if liked. To make the filling, mash 4 bananas in a bowl with 30 ml / 2 tbsp double cream. Stir in a few pieces of chopped preserved ginger.
- **Maple Syrup and Ice Cream** Trickle about 10 ml / 2 tsp maple syrup over each pancake and roll up. Arrange on serving plates and top with good-quality vanilla ice cream.

- **Pineapple** Drain 1 x 227 g / 8 oz can crushed pineapple. Combine the fruit with 250 ml / 8 fl oz soured cream in a bowl. Fill the pancakes with this mixture and serve with a sauce made by heating the fruit syrup with a few drops of lemon juice.
- **Rum Warmers** Place 45 ml / 3 tbsp brown sugar in a saucepan with 5 ml / 1 tsp ground cinnamon and 90 ml / 6 tbsp orange juice. Heat until the sugar melts, then bring to the boil and boil for 1 minute. Remove from the heat and stir in 60 ml / 4 tbsp rum. Moisten the pancakes with a little rum syrup before rolling them up, then trickle the remainder over the top. Serve with whipped cream.
- **Surprise** Spoon ice cream into the centre of each pancake and fold in half like an omelette. Serve at once with Jam Sauce (page 236) or Melba Sauce (page 28).

CHOCOLATE PANCAKE PIE

100 g / 4 oz plain chocolate
50 g / 2 oz icing sugar
whipped cream to serve

PANCAKES
100 g / 4 oz plain flour
1.25 ml / ¼ tsp salt
1 egg, beaten
250 ml / 8 fl oz milk, or half milk and half water
oil for frying

Make the pancakes. Sift the flour and salt into a bowl, make a well in the centre and add the beaten egg. Stir in half the milk (or all the milk, if using a mixture of milk and water), gradually working the flour down from the sides.

Beat vigorously until the mixture is smooth and bubbly, then stir in the rest of the milk (or the water). Pour into a jug. The mixture may be left to stand at this stage, in which case it should be covered and stored in the refrigerator.

Grate the chocolate into a small bowl. Have the icing sugar ready in a sifter. Heat a little oil in a clean 18-cm / 7-inch pancake pan. Pour off any excess oil, leaving the pan covered with a thin film of grease.

Stir the batter and pour about 30–45 ml / 2–3 tbsp into the pan. There should be just enough to cover the base thinly. Tilt and rotate the pan so that the batter runs over the surface evenly.

Cook over moderate heat for about 1 minute until the pancake is set and golden brown underneath. Make sure the pancake is loose by shaking the pan, then either toss it or turn it with a palette knife or fish slice. Cook the second side for about 30 seconds or until golden.

Slide the pancake out on to a warmed plate. Sprinkle generously with grated chocolate and dredge lightly with icing sugar. Cook a second pancake and stack on top of the first, adding a chocolate and icing sugar topping as before. Continue until 8 pancakes have been made and topped. Dredge the top pancake on the stack with icing sugar only.

To serve the pancake pie, cut in wedges and top with whipped cream.

SERVES FOUR

MRS BEETON'S TIP

The chocolate will be easy to grate if it is first chilled in the refrigerator. You can chill the metal grater, too.

CRÊPES SUZETTE

100 g / 4 oz unsalted butter
75 g / 3 oz caster sugar
grated rind and juice of 1 lemon
5 ml / 1 tsp lemon juice
15 ml / 1 tbsp orange liqueur
45 ml / 3 tbsp brandy for flaming

CRÊPES
100 g / 4 oz plain flour
1.25 ml / ¼ tsp salt
1 egg, beaten
250 ml / 8 fl oz milk, or half milk and half water
15 g / ½ oz butter, melted and cooled
oil for frying

Make the crêpe batter. Sift the flour and salt into a bowl, make a well in the centre and add the beaten egg. Stir in half the milk (or all the milk, if using a mixture of milk and water), gradually working the flour down from the sides of the bowl.

Beat vigorously until the mixture is smooth and bubbly, then stir in the rest of the milk (or the water). Pour into a jug. The mixture may be left to stand at this stage, in which case it should be covered and stored in the refrigerator.

Heat a little oil in a clean 18-cm / 7-inch pancake pan. Pour off any excess oil, leaving the pan covered with a thin film of grease.

Stir the melted butter into the batter and pour about 30–45 ml / 2–3 tbsp into the pan. There should be just enough to cover the base thinly. Tilt and rotate the pan so that the batter runs over the surface evenly.

Cook over moderate heat for about 1 minute until the crêpe is set and golden brown underneath. Make sure the crêpe is loose by shaking the pan, then either toss it or turn it with a palette knife or fish slice. Cook the second side for about 30 seconds or until golden.

Slide the crêpe out on to a plate and keep warm over simmering water while making 7 more crêpes in the same way. Add more oil to the pan when necessary.

Make the filling by creaming the unsalted butter with the sugar in a bowl. Beat in the orange rind, lemon juice and liqueur, with enough of the orange juice to give a soft, creamy consistency.

Spread the filling over the cooked crêpes, dividing it evenly between them. Fold each crêpe in half, then in half again to make a quarter circle.

Return half the crêpes to the pan and warm through for 1–2 minutes. As the orange butter melts and runs out, spoon it over the crêpes. Pour in half the brandy, tip the pan to one side and increase the heat. Ignite the brandy and serve at once, with the pan sauce. Repeat with the remaining crêpes and brandy.

SERVES FOUR

APPLE BATTER PUDDING

25 g / 1 oz cooking fat
450 g / 1 lb cooking apples
50 g / 2 oz sugar
grated rind of ½ lemon

BATTER
100 g / 4 oz plain flour
1.25 ml / ¼ tsp salt
1 egg, beaten
250 ml / 8 fl oz milk, or half milk and half water

Make the batter. Sift the flour and salt into a bowl, make a well in the centre and add the beaten egg. Stir in half the milk (or all the milk, if using a mixture of milk and water), gradually working in the flour.

Beat vigorously until the mixture is smooth and bubbly, then stir in the rest of the milk (or the water).

Set the oven at 220°C / 425°F / gas 7. Put the fat into a 28 x 18-cm / 11 x 7-inch baking tin and heat in the oven for 5 minutes.

Meanwhile peel, core and thinly slice the apples. Remove the baking tin from the oven and swiftly arrange the apples on the base. Sprinkle with the sugar and lemon rind. Pour the batter over the top and bake for 30–35 minutes until brown and risen.

Cut into 4 pieces and serve at once, with golden syrup or a Rich Lemon Sauce (page 216) if liked.

SERVES FOUR

VARIATIONS

- **Apricot Batter Pudding** Put 100 g / 4 oz dried apricots in a bowl and add just enough water to cover. Soak until soft, preferably overnight. Transfer the apricots and soaking liquid to a pan and simmer for 15 minutes. Drain.

Make the batter as left, heat the fat, and layer the apricots on the base of the baking tin. Proceed as left. Serve with an apricot jam sauce (page 236).

- **Dried Fruit Batter Pudding** Make the batter and heat the fat as left, then spread 50 g / 2 oz mixed dried fruit over the base of the tin. Sprinkle with 2.5 ml / ½ tsp mixed spice or cinnamon. Proceed as in the main recipe and serve with St Clement's Sauce (page 216).
- **Black Cap Puddings** Make the batter as left. Grease 12 deep patty tins and divide 50 g / 2 oz currants between them. Pour in enough batter to half fill each tin and bake for 15–20 minutes. Turn out to serve, and pass round Ginger Syrup Sauce (page 235).

QUICK BATTER PUDDINGS

Serve poached fruit, such as plums, cherries or apricots, with these puffy puddings.

25 g / 1 oz butter, plus extra for greasing
150 ml / ¼ pint milk
50 g / 2 oz plain flour
25 g / 1 oz caster sugar
grated rind of 1 lemon
1 egg

Set the oven at 220°C / 425°F / gas 7. Butter four ramekin dishes or small baking dishes and place them on a baking sheet.

Heat the butter and milk in a small saucepan until the butter has melted; cool. Mix the flour, sugar and lemon rind in a bowl, then make a well in the centre and add the egg. Add a little milk and beat the egg with a little of the flour mixture. Work in the flour, adding a little of the milk, to make a thick batter and beat until smooth. Gradually beat in the rest of the milk.

Divide the batter between the dishes and bake for 20–30 minutes, until the puddings are risen, golden and set. Serve at once.

SERVES FOUR

APPLE FRITTERS

450 g / 1 lb apples
5 ml / 1 tsp lemon juice
oil for deep frying
caster sugar for sprinkling
St Clement's Sauce (page 216) or
single cream to serve

BATTER
100 g / 4 oz plain flour
1.25 ml / ¼ tsp salt
15 ml / 1 tbsp vegetable oil
60 ml / 4 tbsp milk
2 egg whites

Make the batter. Sift the flour and salt into a bowl. Make a well in the centre of the flour and add the oil and milk. Gradually work in the flour from the sides, then beat well until smooth. Stir in 75 ml / 5 tbsp cold water. The mixture may be left to stand at this stage, in which case it should be covered and stored in the refrigerator.

Peel and core the apples. Cut them into 5-mm / ¼-inch slices and place in a bowl of cold water with the lemon juice added.

Whisk the egg whites in a clean, grease-free bowl until stiff. Give the batter a final beat, then lightly fold in the egg whites.

Set the oven at 150°C / 300°F / gas 2. Put the oil for frying in a deep wide saucepan. Heat the oil to 185°C / 360°F or until a bread cube immersed in the oil turns pale brown in 45 seconds. If using a deep-fat fryer, follow the manufacturer's instructions.

Drain the apples thoroughly and dry with soft absorbent kitchen paper. Coat the apple slices in batter and fry 5 or 6 pieces at a time for 2–3 minutes until golden. Lift out the fritters with a slotted spoon and dry on absorbent kitchen paper. Keep hot on a baking sheet in the oven while cooking the next batch.

When all the fritters have been cooked, sprinkle them with caster sugar and serve with St Clement's Sauce (page 216) or cream.

SERVES FOUR

VARIATIONS

- **Apricot Fritters** Prepare batter as above. Sprinkle drained canned apricot halves with rum and leave for 15 minutes. Coat in batter, then fry. Dredge with caster sugar and serve with custard or cream.
- **Banana Fritters** Prepare batter as above. Peel 4 small bananas, cut in half lengthways, then in half across. Coat in batter, then fry. Serve with custard or liqueur-flavoured cream.
- **Orange Fritters** Prepare batter as above. Remove the peel and pith from 4 oranges. Divide them into pieces of about 2 or 3 segments each. Carefully cut into the centre to remove any pips. Coat in batter, then fry. Serve with custard or cream.
- **Pear Fritters** Prepare batter as above. Peel and core 4 pears. Cut into quarters, sprinkle with sugar and kirsch and leave to stand for 15 minutes. Finely crush 4 almond macaroons and toss the pear pieces in the crumbs. Coat in batter, then fry. Serve with Rich Lemon Sauce (page 216).
- **Pineapple Fritters** Prepare batter as above. Drain 1 x 556 g / 19 oz can pineapple rings, pat dry on absorbent kitchen paper, and sprinkle with 20 ml / 4 tsp kirsch. Leave to stand for 15 minutes. Coat in batter, then fry. Serve with the pineapple juice, thickened with arrowroot.

CLAFOUTI AUX CERISES

There are several versions of this classic French recipe.
If preferred, the cherries may be placed in the dish first,
then all the batter poured over them. Traditionally the stones
are left in the cherries, but it makes for awkward eating.

15 g / ½ oz lard
15 g / ½ oz butter
2 whole eggs, plus 1 egg yolk
75 g / 3 oz granulated sugar
250 ml / 8 fl oz milk
150 g / 5 oz plain flour, sifted
pinch of cinnamon
450 g / 1 lb Morello cherries, stoned
25 g / 1 oz caster sugar
15 ml / 1 tbsp kirsch

Mix the lard with the butter in a small bowl and use to grease an ovenproof dish, about 18 cm / 7 inches in diameter, or a shallow baking tin. Set the oven at 200°C / 400°F / gas 6.

In a bowl, beat the eggs and egg yolk with the sugar until light. Heat the milk in a saucepan until steaming. Gradually blend the flour into the egg mixture alternately with a little of the hot milk to make a batter. Stir in the cinnamon and remaining milk. Pour a thin layer of the batter into the prepared mould and bake for 5–7 minutes. Meanwhile drain the cherries thoroughly on absorbent kitchen paper.

Pour the remaining batter into the mould, add the cherries and sprinkle with caster sugar. Return to the oven for 10 minutes then lower the oven temperature to 190°C / 375°F / gas 5 and cook for 20 minutes more.

Invert the pudding on to a warmed plate. The bottom of the batter should be crusty and the top should resemble thick custard. Serve warm, sprinkled with the kirsch.

SERVES SIX

Steamed Puddings

The steaming-hot puddings in this chapter, from
homely and traditional to light and modern,
are perfect for winter days. Surprise
the family with a steamed sponge
pudding cooked in minutes
in the microwave.

METHODS OF STEAMING

SAUCEPAN AND STEAMER SET

This usually comprises a double-handled saucepan base with one, two or more steamers that fit on top. The steaming sections have perforated bases to allow the steam to pass through and they are slightly smaller in diameter at the bottom to fit neatly into the base. Usually made of stainless steel, this type of steamer may be built up to include several cooking tiers. This is ideal for cooking puddings, and the main course or vegetables for the meal may be cooked in separate tiers at the same time.

BAMBOO STEAMERS

Bamboo steamers with tight-fitting lids are available in different sizes. These are designed to fit in a wok. They are perfect for cooking vegetables, oriental-style dishes and any suitable food which can be placed in a fairly shallow container. Some bamboo steamers are deep enough to hold pudding basins; however most woks will only hold sufficient water for comparatively short periods of steaming and need frequent topping up with boiling water. This type of steamer is not recommended for puddings that require hours of steaming.

EXPANDING STEAMERS

This type of steamer is made from small stainless steel plates that fold up into a compact shape for storage. The steamer opens out as large as is necessary to hold the food. It stands on short legs in the base of a saucepan. The boiling water must be kept below the level of the steamer and the saucepan must have a tight-fitting lid. This type of steamer is ideal for vegetables and it may be used for puddings. Since only a small amount of water may be placed in the pan beneath the steamer it is not suitable for cooking puddings that require many hours of steaming.

ALUMINIUM STEAMERS WITH GRADUATED BASES

These are very common and are designed to fit on top of saucepans of different sizes. Ensure that the steamer has a tight-fitting lid and that it sits neatly on
top of the pan.

ELECTRIC STEAMER

This is a plug-in, work-top appliance. A heating element in the base is thermo-statically controlled to keep the water boiling or steaming at the right tempera-ture. One or two tiers are supplied to fit over the base, with a tight-fitting lid for the top. In comparison with the other types of steamers, this is an expensive option. However, if you intend to steam a lot of foods it may be a worthwhile purchase. Depending on the individual steamer, this type may lose a lot of steam during cooking, creating puddles on the work surface or condensation on surrounding fittings. Check the steaming layers on the base to make sure they fit neatly. Follow the manufacturer's instructions closely.

IMPROVISING

If you do not own a steamer it is possible to steam puddings by standing them in a saucepan and adding boiling water to come part of the way up the outside of the container. Place a suitable saucer or cereal bowl upside down in the bottom of the pan as a base on which to stand the pudding, allowing for a greater depth of water. Make sure that the saucepan has a tight-fitting lid and follow the instructions in individual recipes.

MICROWAVE COOKING

The microwave oven may be used to make excellent steamed puddings. For more information, and a sponge pudding recipe, see Canary Pudding (page 168). Here are some hints for safety and success:

- Never use a metal container or dish with metal trimmings.
- Sponge puddings rise rapidly and to a considerable height, so make sure the basin used is not more than half full before microwave steaming.
- When cooked, sponge puddings should be slightly sticky on top.
- Use microwave cling film or a suitable plate to cover the pudding during cooking.

PRESSURE COOKING

A pressure cooker may be used to cook steamed puddings quickly and very successfully. It may also be used to cook certain other puddings, for example set custards, and notes are given where applicable.

Always read and follow the manufacturer's instructions for your cooker. In particular, check information on the minimum volume of water to use in the cooker, notes about pressure levels and specific advice on cooking sponge-type puddings in the pressure cooker. Selected recipes have been tested in a pressure cooker and timings are given in Pressure Cooker Tips. The following rules should be followed when pressure cooking sponge puddings.

- Traditional recipes for large steamed puddings should be cooked on Low (5 lb) pressure.
- Small puddings and individual puddings may be cooked on High (15 lb) pressure.
- Add at least 900 ml / 1½ pints of water to allow for the pre-steaming time before the cooker is brought to pressure.
- The basin used for the pudding should withstand the temperature reached in the pressure cooker; it should be watertight and not cracked or chipped.
- Thoroughly grease the pudding basin and half or two-thirds fill it.
- Tie down the cover on the basin securely.
- Before bringing to pressure, all sponge puddings must be pre-steamed in boiling water with the lid on but without using weights. This allows the raising agent to work.
- Reduce the pressure slowly after cooking, following the manufacturer's instructions.

TANGY LEMON PUDDING

butter for greasing
50 g / 2 oz plain flour
pinch of salt
5 ml / 1 tsp baking powder
175 g / 6 oz dried white breadcrumbs
100 g / 4 oz caster sugar
100 g / 4 oz shredded suet
grated rind and juice of 2 lemons
2 eggs, beaten
150–175 ml / 5–6 fl oz milk

Grease a 750-ml / 1¼-pint pudding basin. Prepare a steamer or half fill a large saucepan with water and bring to the boil.

Sift the flour, salt and baking powder into a mixing bowl. Stir in the breadcrumbs, sugar, suet and lemon rind. Mix lightly.

In a second bowl, beat the eggs with the lemon juice and about 150 ml / ¼ pint of the milk. Stir into the dry ingredients, adding more milk if necessary to give a soft dropping consistency. Spoon the mixture into the prepared basin, cover with greased greaseproof paper and foil and secure with string.

Put the pudding in the perforated part of the steamer, or stand it on an old saucer or plate in the pan of boiling water. The water should come halfway up the sides of the basin. Cover the pan tightly and steam the pudding over gently simmering water for 1½–2 hours.

Serve from the basin or leave for 5–10 minutes at room temperature to firm up, then turn out on to a serving plate. Serve the pudding with Rich Lemon Sauce (page 216).

SERVES SIX

APRICOT AND ALMOND PUDDING

butter for greasing
75 g / 3 oz butter or margarine
75 g / 3 oz caster sugar
2 eggs, beaten
75 g / 3 oz plain flour
30 ml / 2 tbsp grated orange rind
2.5 ml / ½ tsp baking powder
6 canned apricot halves, chopped
25 g / 1 oz ground almonds
1 slice of orange, halved, to decorate

Grease a 750-ml / 1¼-pint pudding basin. Prepare a steamer or half fill a large saucepan with water and bring to the boil.

Cream the butter or margarine with the sugar in a mixing bowl until light and fluffy. Beat in the eggs gradually, adding a little of the flour if the mixture begins to curdle. Add the orange rind.

Sift the flour and baking powder together and fold lightly into the creamed mixture with the chopped apricots and ground almonds. Spoon the mixture into the prepared basin, cover with greased greaseproof paper and foil and secure with string.

Put the pudding in the perforated part of the steamer, or stand it on an old saucer or plate in the pan of boiling water. The water should come halfway up the sides of the basin. Cover the pan tightly and steam the pudding for 1¼–1½ hours.

Leave for 5 minutes at room temperature to firm up. Turn the pudding out on to a serving plate, decorate with the orange slice and serve with Apricot Sauce (page 228).

SERVES SIX

CUMBERLAND PUDDING

butter for greasing
225 g / 8 oz cooking apples
100 g / 4 oz shredded suet
200 g / 7 oz plain flour
10 ml / 2 tsp baking powder
pinch of salt
150 g / 5 oz currants
75 g / 3 oz soft light brown sugar
1.25 ml / ¼ tsp grated nutmeg
2 eggs, beaten
about 75 ml / 3 fl oz milk
soft light brown sugar for dredging

Peel, core and roughly chop the apples. Put them in a large bowl with the suet, flour, baking powder, salt, currants, brown sugar and nutmeg. Mix well.

Add the beaten eggs with enough milk to make a soft, dropping consistency. Cover the bowl and leave to stand for 1 hour.

Meanwhile grease a 750-ml / 1¼-pint pudding basin. Prepare a steamer or half fill a large saucepan with water; bring to the boil.

Stir the pudding mixture, adding a little more milk if very stiff. Pour the mixture into the basin, cover with greased greaseproof paper and foil and secure with string.

Put the pudding in the perforated part of the steamer, or stand it on an old saucer or plate in the pan of boiling water. The water should come halfway up the sides of the basin. Cover the pan tightly and steam the pudding over gently simmering water for 1¾–2 hours.

Leave the pudding for 5–10 minutes at room temperature to firm up, then turn out on to a serving plate. Dredge with brown sugar before serving.

SERVES FIVE TO SIX

APPLE PUDDING

*It is important to use dried white breadcrumbs, not
fresh breadcrumbs, for this pudding. Dried breadcrumbs
absorb more fruit juice during cooking to give the
cooked pudding the correct consistency.*

**butter for greasing
150 g / 5 oz cooking apples
100 g / 4 oz shredded suet
100 g / 4 oz dried white breadcrumbs
100 g / 4 oz soft light brown sugar
1.25 ml / ¼ tsp grated nutmeg
pinch of salt
2 eggs, beaten
about 125 ml / 4 fl oz milk**

Peel, core and roughly chop the apples. Mix them in a large bowl with the suet,
breadcrumbs, sugar, nutmeg and salt.

Add the beaten eggs with enough milk to make a soft, dropping consistency.
Leave to stand for 1 hour.

Meanwhile grease a 1-litre / 1¾-pint pudding basin. Prepare a steamer or half
fill a large saucepan with water and bring to the boil.

Stir the mixture, adding a little more milk if very stiff. Pour the mixture into the
basin, cover with greased greaseproof paper and foil and secure with string.

Put the pudding in the perforated part of the steamer, or stand it on an old saucer
or plate in the pan of boiling water. The water should come halfway up the sides
of the basin. Cover the pan tightly and steam the pudding over gently simmering water for 1¾–2 hours.

Serve from the basin or leave for 5–10 minutes at room temperature to firm up,
then turn out on to a serving plate.

SERVES FIVE TO SIX

VARIATIONS

- The recipe works equally well with a wide variety of other fruits. Try damsons, gooseberries, greengages, plums or rhubarb, adjusting the quantity of sugar as required.

PRESSURE COOKER TIP

Pour 900 ml / 1½ pints boiling water into the pressure cooker. Stand the pudding on the trivet and steam it with the lid on, without weights, for 10 minutes. Bring to 15 lb pressure and cook for 25 minutes. Reduce pressure slowly.

GOLDEN SYRUP PUDDING

butter for greasing
45 ml / 3 tbsp golden syrup
150 g / 5 oz plain flour
5 ml / 1 tsp bicarbonate of soda
pinch of salt
5 ml / 1 tsp ground ginger
150 g / 5 oz dried white breadcrumbs
100 g / 4 oz shredded suet
50 g / 2 oz caster sugar
1 egg
15 ml / 1 tbsp black treacle
75–100 ml / 3–3½ fl oz milk

Grease a 1-litre / 1¾-pint pudding basin and put 15 ml / 1 tbsp golden syrup in the bottom. Prepare a steamer or half fill a large saucepan with water and bring to the boil.

Sift the flour, bicarbonate of soda, salt and ginger into a mixing bowl. Add the breadcrumbs, suet and sugar and mix lightly.

In a second bowl, combine the egg, remaining syrup and treacle. Beat in 75 ml / 3 fl oz of the milk. Stir into the dry ingredients, adding more milk if necessary to give a soft dropping consistency.

Spoon the mixture into the prepared basin, cover with greased greaseproof paper and foil and secure with string.

Put the pudding in the perforated part of the steamer, or stand it on an old saucer or plate in the pan of boiling water. The water should come halfway up the sides of the basin. Cover the pan tightly and steam the pudding over gently simmering water for 1½–2 hours.

Leave for 5–10 minutes at room temperature to firm up, then turn out on to a serving plate. Serve with additional warmed golden syrup as a sauce and whipped cream.

SERVES SIX TO EIGHT

SPOTTED DICK

butter for greasing
300 g / 10 oz plain flour
15 ml / 1 tbsp baking powder
150 g / 5 oz shredded suet or suet substitute
75 g / 3 oz caster sugar
100 g / 4 oz currants
finely grated zest of 2 lemons
200 ml / 7 fl oz milk

Grease a 1-litre / 1¾-pint pudding basin. Prepare a steamer or half fill a large saucepan with water and bring to the boil.

Mix the dry ingredients with the currants and lemon zest. Add most of the milk, adding up to 200 ml / 7 fl oz until the mixture is of a soft, dropping consistency.

Spoon the mixture into the prepared basin, cover with greased greaseproof paper and foil and secure with string.

Put the pudding in the perforated part of the steamer, or stand it on an old saucer or plate in the pan of boiling water. The water should come halfway up the sides of the basin. Cover the pan tightly and steam the pudding over gently simmering water for 1 hour.

Serve from the basin or leave for 5–10 minutes at room temperature to firm up, then turn out on to a serving plate. Serve with custard or double cream.

SERVES SIX TO EIGHT

CABINET PUDDING

butter for greasing
75 g / 3 oz seedless raisins, halved
3–4 slices of white bread, crusts removed
400 ml / 14 fl oz milk
3 eggs
25 g / 1 oz caster sugar
5 ml / 1 tsp grated lemon rind

Grease a 1-litre / 1¾-pint pudding basin. Decorate the sides and base of the basin by pressing on some of the halved raisins. Chill.

Cut the bread slices into 5-mm / ¼-inch dice and place in a bowl. In a saucepan, warm the milk to about 65°C / 150°F; do not let it come near to the boil.

Meanwhile mix the eggs and sugar in a bowl. Beat with a fork and stir in the milk, with the lemon rind and remaining raisins. Pour the custard mixture over the bread, stir, and leave to stand for at least 30 minutes. Meanwhile prepare a steamer or half fill a large saucepan with water and bring to the boil.

Spoon the bread mixture into the prepared basin, cover with greased grease-proof paper or foil and secure with string.

Put the pudding in the perforated part of the steamer, or stand it on an old saucer or plate in the pan of boiling water. The water should come halfway up the sides of the basin.

FREEZER TIP

Crumb the bread crusts in a food processor and store in a polythene bag in the freezer. Next time you make a fruit pie, sprinkle a thin layer of crumbs into the pie shell before adding the fruit; they will prevent the fruit juices from making the crust soggy.

Cover the pan tightly and steam the pudding over gently simmering water for 1 hour or until firm in the centre.

Remove the cooked pudding from the steamer, leave to stand for a few minutes, then turn out on to a warmed serving dish. Serve with a jam or fruit sauce.

SERVES FOUR TO SIX

PADDINGTON PUDDING

butter for greasing
100 g / 4 oz dried white breadcrumbs
100 g / 4 oz sultanas
100 g / 4 oz shredded suet
100 g / 4 oz self-raising flour
grated rind of 1 lemon
50 g / 2 oz caster sugar
pinch of salt
60 ml / 4 tbsp marmalade
2 eggs, beaten
about 75 ml / 3 fl oz milk

Grease a 1-litre / 1¾-pint pudding basin. Prepare a steamer or half fill a large saucepan with water and bring to the boil.

Mix the breadcrumbs, sultanas, suet, flour, grated rind, sugar, salt and marmalade in a mixing bowl. Stir in the beaten eggs with enough milk to give a dropping consistency. Spoon the mixture into the prepared basin, cover with greased greaseproof paper and foil and secure with string.

Put the pudding in the perforated part of the steamer, or stand it on an old saucer or plate in the pan of boiling water. The water should come halfway up the sides of the basin. Cover the pan tightly and steam the pudding over gently simmering water for 1½–2 hours. Leave for 5–10 minutes at room temperature to firm up, then turn out on to a serving plate. Serve with single cream or custard.

SERVES SIX

RICH CHRISTMAS PUDDING

butter for greasing
225 g / 8 oz plain flour
pinch of salt
5 ml / 1 tsp ground ginger
5 ml / 1 tsp mixed spice
5 ml / 1 tsp grated nutmeg
50 g / 2 oz blanched almonds, chopped
400 g / 14 oz soft dark brown sugar
225 g / 8 oz shredded suet
225 g / 8 oz sultanas
225 g / 8 oz currants
200 g / 7 oz seedless raisins
175 g / 6 oz cut mixed peel
175 g / 6 oz dried white breadcrumbs
6 eggs
75 ml / 5 tbsp stout
juice of 1 orange
50 ml / 2 fl oz brandy
125–250 ml / 4–8 fl oz milk

Grease four 600-ml / 1-pint pudding basins. Three-quarters fill four saucepans, each deep enough to hold a single pudding, with water.

Sift the flour, salt, ginger, mixed spice and nutmeg into a very large mixing bowl. Add the almonds, sugar, suet, dried fruit, peel and breadcrumbs.

In a second bowl, combine the eggs, stout, orange juice, brandy and 125 ml / 4 fl oz milk. Mix well.

Stir the liquid mixture into the dry ingredients, adding more milk if necessary to give a soft dropping consistency. Divide the mixture between the pudding basins, covering each with greased greaseproof paper and a floured cloth or foil. Secure with string.

Carefully lower the basins into the pans of boiling water. Cover the pans and lower the heat so that the water is kept at a steady simmer.

Cook the puddings for 6–7 hours, topping up each pan with boiling water as required. The pudding basins should be covered at all times with boiling water.

To store, cover each pudding with a clean dry cloth, wrap in greaseproof paper and store in a cool, dry place until required. To reheat, boil or steam each pudding for 1½–2 hours. Serve with Brandy Butter (page 237) or Brandy and Almond Butter (page 238).

EACH PUDDING SERVES SIX

STORING CHRISTMAS PUDDING

The large quantity of sugar and dried fruit together act as a preservative in Christmas pudding. After cooking, make sure that the pudding is dry and wrap it in clean paper, then place it in an airtight container or seal it in a polythene bag. Foil may be used as an outer covering, over paper, but it should not come in direct contact with the pudding as the fruit acid causes it to break down and disintegrate to a coarse foil powder which ruins the surface of the pudding. Kept in a cool, dry, place, Christmas pudding will remain excellent for up to a year. 'Feed' it occasionally with a little brandy.

PRESSURE COOKER TIP

Pour 1.5 litres / 2½ pints boiling water into the pressure cooker. Stand one pudding on the trivet and steam it, without weights, for 20 minutes. Bring to 15 1b pressure and cook for 1¾ hours. Allow the pressure to reduce slowly. To reheat, cook at 15 1b pressure for 20 minutes, reduce pressure slowly and serve.

PLUM PUDDING

*Christmas pudding became known as plum pudding
in Tudor times, when dried plums (prunes)
were the popular prime ingredient.*

butter for greasing
100 g / 4 oz cooking apple
200 g / 7 oz dried figs, chopped
100 g / 4 oz currants
225 g / 8 oz seedless raisins
200 g / 7 oz blanched almonds, chopped
25 g / 1 oz shelled Brazil nuts, chopped
100 g / 4 oz pine kernels
175 g / 6 oz dried white breadcrumbs
5 ml / 1 tsp mixed spice
100 g / 4 oz soft light brown sugar
100 g / 4 oz cut mixed peel
pinch of salt
grated rind and juice of 1 lemon
100 g / 4 oz butter or margarine
100 g / 4 oz honey
3 eggs, beaten

Grease two 750-ml / 1¼-pint pudding basins. Prepare two steamers or three-quarter fill two saucepans with water. Each pan should hold one pudding.

Peel, core and chop the apple. Put it in a large mixing bowl with the dried fruits, nuts, breadcrumbs, spice, sugar, peel, salt and the lemon rind and juice.

Combine the butter and honey in a saucepan and warm gently until the butter has melted. Beat in the eggs.

Stir the liquid mixture into the dry ingredients and mix well. Spoon the mixture into the basins, cover with greased greaseproof paper and a floured cloth or foil. Secure with string.

Place the basins in the steamers or carefully lower them into the pans of boiling water. Cover the pans and lower the heat so that the water is kept at a steady simmer. Boil the puddings for 3 hours or steam for 3½–4 hours, topping up each pan with boiling water as required.

To store, cover each pudding with a clean dry cloth, wrap in greaseproof paper and store in a cool, dry place until required. To reheat, boil or steam each pudding for 1½–2 hours.

EACH PUDDING SERVES SIX

MRS BEETON'S TIP

Plum puddings are traditionally flamed when served. To do this, warm 30–45 ml / 2–3 tbsp brandy, either in a soup ladle over a low flame or in a measuring jug in the microwave for 15 seconds on High. Ignite the brandy (if warmed in a soup ladle it may well ignite spontaneously) and carefully pour it over the hot pudding. Do not use holly to decorate the top of a pudding that is to be flamed.

CANARY PUDDING

butter for greasing
150 g / 5 oz butter or margarine
150 g / 5 oz caster sugar
3 eggs, beaten
150 g / 5 oz plain flour
grated rind of ½ lemon
5 ml / 1 tsp baking powder

Grease a 1-litre / 1¾-pint pudding basin. Prepare a steamer or half fill a large saucepan with water and bring to the boil.

Cream the butter or margarine with the sugar in a mixing bowl until light and fluffy. Beat in the eggs gradually, adding a little of the flour if the mixture begins to curdle. Add the lemon rind.

Sift the flour and baking powder together and fold lightly into the creamed mixture. Spoon the mixture into the prepared basin, cover with greased grease-proof paper and foil and secure with string.

Put the pudding in the perforated part of the steamer, or stand it on an old saucer or plate in the pan of boiling water. The water should come halfway up the sides of the basin. Cover the pan tightly and steam the pudding over gently simmering water for 1¼–1½ hours. Leave for 3–5 minutes at room temperature to firm up, then turn out on to a serving plate.

SERVES SIX

MICROWAVE TIP

*To make a light sponge pudding in the microwave,
use 50 g / 2 oz each of butter or margarine,
sugar and self-raising flour with 1 egg and
30 ml / 2 tbsp milk. Prepare the pudding as above
and put it into a greased 1.1-litre / 2-pint basin.
Cook on High for 3–5 minutes.*

VARIATIONS

- **Date Sponge Pudding** Add 150 g / 5 oz chopped stoned dates. Substitute orange rind for lemon rind.
- **Dried Fruit Sponge Pudding** Add to the basic recipe 150 g / 5 oz mixed dried fruit. Serve with a vanilla custard.
- **Chocolate Sponge Pudding** Substitute 25 g / 1 oz cocoa for the same quantity of the flour and stir 75 g / 3 oz chocolate chips into the mixture.
- **Ginger Sponge Pudding** Add 10 ml / 2 tsp ground ginger with the flour and stir 50 g / 2 oz chopped preserved ginger into the mixture.

PARADISE PUDDING

butter for greasing
**225 g / 8 oz cooking apples, peeled, cored
and minced**
3 eggs, beaten
75 g / 3 oz sugar
75 g / 3 oz currants
grated rind of 1 lemon
100 g / 4 oz fresh white breadcrumbs
2.5 ml / ½ tsp grated nutmeg
60 ml / 4 tbsp brandy

Grease a 1-litre / 1¾-pint soufflé dish or basin. Prepare a steamer or half fill a large saucepan with water and bring to the boil.

Mix all the ingredients in a bowl and beat well. Turn into the dish, cover with greased greaseproof paper and foil and secure with string. Put the pudding in the perforated part of the steamer, or stand it on an old saucer or plate in the pan of boiling water. Steam over boiling water for 1¼ hours, until set to the middle. Serve with a vanilla custard.

SERVES SIX

TREACLE LAYER PUDDING

butter for greasing
65 g / 2½ oz dried white breadcrumbs
grated rind of 1 lemon
200 g / 7 oz treacle or golden syrup or a mixture

SUET CRUST PASTRY
300 g / 11 oz plain flour pinch of salt
10 ml / 2 tsp baking powder
150 g / 5 oz shredded suet
flour for rolling out

Grease a 1-litre / 1¾-pint pudding basin. Prepare a steamer or half fill a large saucepan with water and bring to the boil.

Make the pastry. Sift the flour, salt and baking powder into a mixing bowl. Add the suet and enough cold water (about 250 ml / 8 fl oz) to make an elastic dough. Divide the dough in two equal portions.

On a floured surface, roll out one portion of the suet pastry to a round 1 cm / ½ inch larger than the top of the prepared pudding basin. Put the pastry into the basin and, pressing with the fingers, ease it evenly up the sides to the top.

Use half the remaining pastry to make a lid to fit the top of the basin. Thinly roll out the rest and cut two rounds in graduated sizes to fit the basin at two different levels.

In a bowl, mix the breadcrumbs and lemon rind. Put a layer of treacle or golden syrup on the base of the pastry-lined basin and sprinkle generously with the breadcrumb mixture. Cover with the smaller pastry round, moistening the edges with water and pressing them to join them to the pastry at the side of the basin. Layer the remaining ingredients and pastry, finishing with the pastry lid.

Cover the pudding with greased greaseproof paper and foil and secure with string. Put the pudding in the perforated part of the steamer or stand it on an old saucer or plate in the pan of boiling water. The water should come halfway up the sides of the basin. Cover the pan tightly and steam the pudding over gently simmering water for 2¼–2½ hours.

Serve from the basin or leave for 5–10 minutes at room temperature to firm up, then turn out on to a serving plate. Serve with warmed golden syrup and single cream.

SERVES SIX TO EIGHT

VICARAGE PUDDING

Pepped up with orange and adapted to use less suet
or block margarine, this is delicious.

butter for greasing
175 g / 6 oz self-raising flour
50 g / 2 oz suet or block margarine, chilled and grated
100 g / 4 oz currants
50 g / 2 oz soft light brown sugar
5 ml / 1 tsp ground ginger
grated rind and juice of 1 orange
about 50 ml / 2 fl oz milk (see method)

Grease a 1-litre / 1¾-pint pudding basin. Prepare a steamer or half fill a large saucepan with water and bring to the boil.

Beat all the ingredients together in a mixing bowl until thoroughly combined, adding a little milk, if necessary to give the mixture a firm dropping consistency.

Turn into the prepared pudding basin. Cover with greaseproof paper and foil and secure with string. Put the pudding in the perforated part of the steamer, or stand it on an old saucer or plate in the pan of boiling water. Cover the pan tightly and steam the pudding over simmering water for 1½ hours. Serve piping hot with a vanilla custard or cream.

SERVES FOUR TO SIX

HOUSE OF COMMONS PUDDING

butter for greasing
50 g / 2 oz seedless raisins
30 ml / 2 tbsp medium sherry
4 trifle sponges
9 ratafias or 2 almond macaroons
400 ml / 14 fl oz milk
3 eggs
25 g / 1 oz caster sugar
few drops of vanilla essence

DECORATION
glacé cherries, halved
angelica, cut in strips

Put the raisins in a small bowl with the sherry and macerate for 15 minutes. Meanwhile grease a 13-cm / 5-inch round cake tin and line the base with greased greaseproof paper. Decorate the base of the tin with the cherries and angelica.

Cut the sponges into 1-cm / ½-inch dice and put into a bowl. Add the crumbled rataflas or macaroons and mix lightly. Drain the raisins, discarding the sherry.

Add a layer of the sponge mixture to the prepared tin, taking care not to spoil the design. Top with a few of the drained raisins. Repeat the layers until all the sponge mixture and raisins have been used.

In a saucepan, bring the milk to just below boiling point. Put the eggs and sugar into a bowl, mix well, then stir in the scalded milk. Add a few drops of vanilla essence. Slowly strain the custard mixture into the cake tin, allowing it to seep down to the base of the tin gradually, so as not to disturb the pattern on the base. Leave to stand for 1 hour.

Prepare a steamer or half fill a large saucepan with water and bring to the boil. Cover the cake tin with greased greaseproof paper or foil and secure with string. Put the pudding in the perforated part of the steamer, or stand it on an old saucer or plate in the pan of boiling water. The water should come halfway up the sides of the cake tin. Cover the pan tightly and steam the pudding over gently simmering water for 1 hour.

Remove the pudding from the steamer, leave to stand for a few minutes, then turn out on to a warmed dish and peel off the lining paper. Serve with Sabayon Sauce (page 226), if liked.

SERVES FOUR

SAXON PUDDING

Trifle sponges can be used in this pudding; however, far better results are obtained by using home-made cake or good-quality bought plain cake. If you have difficulty in obtaining ratafias, use double the quantity of almond macaroons instead.

oil for greasing
glacé cherries
angelica
25 g / 1 oz flaked almonds
3 slices of plain cake or trifle sponges, crumbed
4 almond macaroons, crumbed
12 ratafias
2 eggs
100 ml / 3½ fl oz single cream
25 g / 1 oz caster sugar
300 ml / ½ pint milk
45 ml / 3 tbsp sherry

Grease a 13-cm / 5-inch round cake tin and line the base with oiled greaseproof paper. Cut the cherries and angelica into small shapes and arrange them in a decorative pattern on the base of the prepared cake tin.

Spread out the almonds on a baking sheet and place under a hot grill for a few minutes until browned. Shake the sheet from time to time and watch the almonds carefully as they will readily scorch. Use the almonds to decorate the sides of the greased cake tin.

Mix the cake and macaroon crumbs with the ratafias in a mixing bowl. In a second bowl, combine the eggs, cream and sugar. Mix lightly, then stir in the milk. Strain on to the crumb mixture and add the sherry. Stir, then leave to stand for 1 hour.

Meanwhile prepare a steamer or half fill a large saucepan with water and bring to the boil. Stir the pudding mixture again, making sure the ratafias are properly soaked. Spoon the mixture into the prepared cake tin, taking care not to spoil the decoration. Cover with greased greaseproof paper or foil and secure with string.

Put the pudding in the perforated part of the steamer, or stand it on an old saucer or plate in the pan of boiling water. The water should come halfway up the sides of the tin. Cover the pan tightly and steam the pudding over gently simmering water for 1–1¼ hours.

Remove the cooked pudding from the steamer, leave to stand for 5–10 minutes at room temperature to firm up, then turn out on to a warmed serving plate. Peel off the lining paper. Serve hot, with Thickened Fruit Sauce (page 229) or cold with whipped cream.

SERVES FOUR

PRESSURE COOKER TIP

*Pour 900 ml / 1½ pints boiling water
into the cooker. Cook the pudding
at 15 lb pressure for 10 minutes.
Reduce pressure slowly.*

GINGER PUDDING

butter for greasing
200 g / 7 oz plain flour
5 ml / 1 tsp ground ginger
pinch of salt
5 ml / 1 tsp bicarbonate of soda
100 g / 4 oz shredded suet
75 g / 3 oz caster sugar
15 ml / 1 tbsp black treacle
1 egg, beaten
50–100 ml / 2–3½ fl oz milk

Grease a 1-litre / 1¾-pint pudding basin. Prepare a steamer or half fill a large saucepan with water and bring to the boil.

Sift the flour, ginger, salt and bicarbonate of soda into a mixing bowl. Add the suet and sugar. Mix lightly.

In a second bowl, beat the treacle and egg with 50 ml / 2 fl oz of the milk. Stir the liquid mixture into the dry ingredients, adding more milk if necessary to give a soft dropping consistency.

Spoon the mixture into the prepared basin, cover with greased greaseproof paper and foil and secure with string.

Put the pudding in the perforated part of the steamer, or stand it on an old saucer or plate in the pan of boiling water. The water should come halfway up the sides of the basin. Cover the pan tightly and steam the pudding over gently simmering water for 1¾–2 hours.

Serve from the basin or leave for 5–10 minutes at room temperature to firm up, then turn out on to a serving plate. Serve with Ginger Syrup Sauce (page 235) or Classic Egg Custard Sauce (page 222).

SERVES SIX

CHOCOLATE CRUMB PUDDING

The mixture is particularly suitable for making individual puddings and the results are so light that they are ideal for 'dressing up' for dinner party occasions. Simple finishing touches, such as cream feathered through the sauce, or serving fresh fruit with the puddings, make the dinner party dessert very special.

butter for greasing
50 g / 2 oz plain chocolate
125 ml / 4 fl oz milk
40 g / 1½ oz butter or margarine
40 g / 1½ oz caster sugar
2 eggs, separated
100 g / 4 oz dried white breadcrumbs
1.25 ml / ¼ tsp baking powder

DECORATION
Chocolate Caraque (see opposite) or grated chocolate
strawberries, halved (optional)

Grease a 750-ml / 1¼-pint pudding basin or six dariole moulds. Prepare a steamer or half fill a large saucepan with water and bring to the boil.

Grate the chocolate into a saucepan, add the milk and heat slowly to melt the chocolate. Cream the butter or margarine with the sugar in a mixing bowl. Beat in the egg yolks with the melted chocolate mixture. Add the breadcrumbs and baking powder.

In a clean, grease-free bowl, whisk the egg whites until fairly stiff. Fold them into the pudding mixture. Spoon the mixture into the prepared basin or dariole moulds, cover with greased greaseproof paper and foil, and secure with string.

Put the pudding or puddings in the perforated part of the steamer, or stand it (them) on an old plate in the pan of boiling water. The water should come halfway up the sides of the basin or moulds. Cover the pan tightly and steam the pudding over gently simmering water for 1 hour for a large pudding, or 30 minutes for individual moulds.

Leave for 3–5 minutes at room temperature to firm up, then turn out on to a serving plate. Serve with Chocolate Cream Sauce (page 231), Mocha Sauce (page 232) or whipped cream. Top the puddings with chocolate caraque or grated chocolate and decorate with fresh strawberries when in season.

SERVES SIX

MAKING CHOCOLATE CURLS (CARAQUE)

Pour melted chocolate over a clean, dry, cool and flat surface. Spread the chocolate backwards and forwards with a large palette knife until it is smooth, fairly thin and even. Leave until almost set but do not allow the chocolate to set hard.

Hold a long, thin-bladed knife at an acute angle to the chocolate. Hold the top of the knife with the other hand and pull the knife towards you with a gentle sawing action, scraping off a thin layer of chocolate that curls into a roll.

MRS BEETON'S TIP

Feather a little single cream through the sauce. Put a few drops of cream on to the chocolate or mocha sauce, then drag the tip of a cocktail stick through it.

EVERYDAY CHOCOLATE PUDDING

butter for greasing
200 g / 7 oz plain flour
5 ml / 1 tsp baking powder
pinch of salt
25 g / 1 oz cocoa
100 g / 4 oz butter or margarine
100 g / 4 oz caster sugar
2 eggs
1.25 ml / ¼ tsp vanilla essence
milk (see method)

Grease a 1-litre / 1¾-pint pudding basin. Prepare a steamer or half fill a large saucepan with water and bring to the boil.

Sift the flour, baking powder, salt and cocoa into a mixing bowl. Rub in the butter or margarine and stir in the sugar.

In a second bowl, beat the eggs with the vanilla essence. Add to the dry ingredients with enough milk to give a soft dropping consistency. Spoon the mixture into the prepared basin, cover with greased greaseproof paper and foil and secure with string. Put the pudding in the perforated part of the steamer, or stand it on an old saucer or plate in the pan of boiling water. The water should come halfway up the sides of the basin. Cover the pan tightly and steam the pudding over gently simmering water for 1¾–2 hours.

MRS BEETON'S TIP

When rubbing the fat into the flour, use only the tips of your fingers, lifting the mixture above the surface of the bowl and letting it drop back naturally to incorporate as much air as possible.

Leave for 5–10 minutes at room temperature to firm up, then turn out on to a serving plate. Serve with Mocha Sauce (page 232) or, on special occasions, with Chocolate Liqueur Sauce (page 232).

SERVES SIX

CLOUTIE DUMPLING

300 g / 11 oz self-raising flour
5 ml / 1 tsp baking powder
100 g / 4 oz shredded suet
5 ml / 1 tsp mixed spice
5 ml / 1 tsp ground ginger
5 ml / 1 tsp ground cinnamon
2.5 ml / ½ tsp salt
100 g / 4 oz soft light brown sugar
50 g / 2 oz muscatel raisins, seeded
100 g / 4 oz sultanas
50 g / 2 oz cut mixed peel
1 carrot, grated
100 g / 4 oz black treacle
200 ml / 7 fl oz milk
1 egg, beaten
flour for dusting and butter for greasing

Mix the flour, baking powder, suet, spices, salt and sugar in a mixing bowl. Stir in the raisins, sultanas and mixed peel with the carrot.

Put the treacle in a saucepan with the milk and dissolve over low heat. Stir into the dry ingredients with the egg to give a fairly soft dropping consistency. Mix thoroughly.

Put the mixture into a scalded and floured cloth and tie with string, allowing room for expansion. Place on a plate in a pan and add sufficient boiling water to come three-quarters of the way up the dumpling. Simmer for 3 hours.

Alternatively spoon the mixture into a greased 1.5-litre / 2½-pint basin, cover with greased greaseproof paper and foil and secure with string. Cook in a steamer or on an old saucer or plate in a pan of boiling water. The water should come halfway up the sides of the basin. Simmer as above.

Turn out on to a serving dish and serve hot or cold with Classic Egg Custard Sauce (page 222) or Sweet Sherry Sauce (page 236).

SERVES FOUR TO SIX

MRS BEETON'S TIP

To save transferring the sticky treacle, measure it in the saucepan, weighing the empty pan first and then adding sufficient treacle to increase the weight by 100 g / 4 oz.

PATRIOTIC PUDDING

butter for greasing
45 ml / 3 tbsp red jam
200 g / 7 oz plain flour
pinch of salt
10 ml / 2 tsp baking powder
100 g / 4 oz butter or margarine
100 g / 4 oz caster sugar
1 egg, beaten
about 75 ml / 3 fl oz milk

Grease a 1-litre / 1¾-pint pudding basin and cover the base with the jam. Prepare a steamer or half fill a large saucepan with water and bring to the boil.

Sift the flour, salt and baking powder into a mixing bowl. Rub in the butter or margarine and add the sugar. Stir in the egg and milk to give a soft dropping consistency. Spoon the mixture into the prepared basin, cover with greased greaseproof paper and foil and secure with string.

Put the pudding in the perforated part of the steamer, or stand it on an old saucer or plate in the pan of boiling water. The water should come halfway up the sides of the basin. Cover the pan tightly and steam the pudding over gently simmering water for 1½–2 hours.

SERVES SIX

PRESSURE COOKER TIP

Pour 1.1 litres / 2 pints boiling water into the cooker. Steam the pudding without weights on the cooker for 15 minutes. Bring to 15 lb pressure and cook for 25 minutes. Reduce pressure slowly.

BACHELOR PUDDING

butter for greasing
1 cooking apple (about 150 g / 5 oz)
100 g / 4 oz dried white breadcrumbs
grated rind of ½ lemon
100 g / 4 oz currants
75 g / 3 oz caster sugar
pinch of salt
1.25 ml / ¼ tsp grated nutmeg
2 eggs, beaten
125 ml / 4 fl oz milk
2.5 ml / ½ tsp baking powder

Peel, core and grate the apple. Put it into a mixing bowl with the breadcrumbs, lemon rind, currants, sugar, salt and nutmeg. Add the eggs with enough of the milk to give a soft dropping consistency. Leave to stand for 30 minutes.

Grease a 1-litre / 1¾-pint pudding basin. Prepare a steamer or half fill a large saucepan with water and bring to the boil.

Stir the baking powder into the pudding mixture. Spoon the mixture into the prepared basin, cover with greased greaseproof paper and foil and secure with string.

Put the pudding in the perforated part of the steamer, or stand it on an old saucer or plate in the pan of boiling water. The water should come halfway up the sides of the basin. Cover the pan tightly and steam the pudding over gently simmering water for 2½–3 hours.

Serve from the basin or leave for 5–10 minutes at room temperature to firm up, then turn out on to a serving plate. Serve with Redcurrant Sauce (page 214) or Cold Chantilly Apple Sauce (page 230).

SERVES SIX

Cobblers & Baked Puddings

*These puddings combine seasonal
fruits with hearty toppings and
light crumbly coverings.*

COBBLERS

A cobbler is usually a fruit pudding with a topping of sweet scone dough. The basic scone mixture is made of self-raising flour (or plain flour with baking powder, or a mixture of bicarbonate of soda and cream of tartar) with a little fat and sugar. The dry ingredients are bound with milk.

Scone dough should be soft but not too sticky and it should be kneaded very lightly into a smooth ball before it is rolled out. It should not be handled heavily or for too long, otherwise the result will be heavy.

CRUMBLES

Crumbles are quick and easy to make and the basic mixture of flour, fat and sugar may be varied in many ways. Spices, nuts and cereals may be stirred in to add texture and flavour to the cooked crumble. When served, the topping should be browned and crisp, crumbly and cooked through.

Handle the crumble mixture lightly, sprinkling it over the fruit and spreading it evenly without pressing down too firmly.

FREEZING

Both cobblers and crumbles freeze well. The scone topping for cobblers must be cooked before freezing. The complete cobbler may be frozen or prepared scone toppings may be frozen separately for thawing and reheating on a base of cooked fruit.

Crumbles may be frozen when cooked or may be prepared ready for cooking, frozen and cooked just before serving. Alternatively, the raw crumble mix may be frozen in a suitable bag, ready to be sprinkled over the fruit before cooking.

If you are freezing a pudding in its dish, make sure that the dish is suitable.

OTHER BAKED PUDDINGS

As well as puddings with crumble or cobbler toppings, this chapter offers recipes for fruits cooked with sponge or meringue toppings. There are light mixtures baked with fruit and other flavourings or substantial puddings using bread. A recipe for a self-saucing lemon pudding is also featured: a light cake batter separates during baking to give a delicate spongy top with a tangy lemon sauce below. In addition there are a few classic British puddings and others that make the most of tart cooking apples, such as Bramleys.

PEAR AND ORANGE COBBLER

This is an excellent pudding for using up a glut of home-grown pears.

grated rind and juice of 2 large oranges
30 ml / 2 tbsp clear honey
5 ml / 1 tsp cornflour
8 ripe pears, peeled, cored and sliced

TOPPING
175 g / 6 oz plain wholemeal flour
15 ml / 1 tbsp baking powder
50 g / 2 oz butter or margarine
50 g / 2 oz soft light brown sugar
75 g / 3 oz walnuts, chopped
about 75 ml / 3 fl oz milk, plus extra to glaze

Set the oven at 230°C / 450°F / gas 8. Combine the orange rind and juice in a small saucepan. Stir in the honey and cornflour. Heat gently until boiling, stirring all the time. Lower the heat, add the pears and poach them for 2–5 minutes or until tender. Transfer the mixture to an ovenproof dish.

Make the topping. Mix the flour and baking powder in a bowl, then rub in the butter until the mixture resembles fine breadcrumbs. Stir in the sugar and walnuts. Mix in enough milk to make a soft dough.

Turn the dough out on to a lightly floured surface and knead it very lightly into a ball. Roll or pat out to an 18-cm / 7-inch round and cut this into equal wedges.

Arrange the scone wedges, set slightly apart, on top of the pears and brush the top of the dough with a little milk. Bake for about 15 minutes, until the scones are well risen and browned. Serve the cobbler freshly cooked, with a vanilla custard.

SERVES SIX

APPLE AND BANANA COBBLER

900 g / 2 lb cooking apples
75–100 g / 3–4 oz sugar
50 g / 2 oz raisins

TOPPING
225 g / 8 oz self-raising flour
5 ml / 1 tsp baking powder
50 g / 2 oz butter or margarine
50 g / 2 oz sugar, plus extra for sprinkling
1 banana
about 125 ml / 4 fl oz milk, plus extra for brushing

Peel and core the apples. Slice them into a saucepan and add the sugar, raisins and 30 ml / 2 tbsp water. Cook gently, stirring occasionally, until the apples are just soft. Transfer to an ovenproof dish.

Set the oven at 230°C / 450°F / gas 8. Make the topping. Sift the flour and baking powder into a bowl. Rub in the butter or margarine until the mixture resembles fine breadcrumbs, then stir in the sugar. Peel and slice the banana and add to the mixture, with enough milk to bind the dough.

Turn the dough out on to a lightly floured surface and knead it very lightly into a smooth ball. Cut the dough into quarters, then cut each piece in half to make eight scones. Flatten each portion of dough into a round about 5 cm / 2 inches in diameter.

Place the scones around the edge of the dish on top of the apples, overlapping them slightly. Brush the scones with a little milk and sprinkle them with sugar.

Bake the cobbler in the preheated oven for about 15 minutes, until the scones are well risen and browned.

SERVES SIX TO EIGHT

GOOSEBERRY COBBLER

450 g / 1 lb gooseberries, topped and tailed
100 g / 4 oz sugar

TOPPING
100 g / 4 oz self-raising flour
25 g / 1 oz margarine
about 60 ml / 4 tbsp milk, plus extra for brushing
40 g / 1½ oz glacé cherries, chopped
40 g / 1½ oz blanched almonds, chopped
30 ml / 2 tbsp sugar

Place the gooseberries in a saucepan with the sugar. Cook gently, stirring occasionally, until the fruit is soft. Transfer to an ovenproof dish.

Set the oven at 220°C / 425°F / gas 7. Sift the flour into a bowl and rub in the margarine until the mixture resembles fine breadcrumbs. Stir in enough milk to make a soft dough.

In a small bowl, mix the cherries with the almonds and sugar. Turn the dough out on to a lightly floured surface and knead it gently into a smooth ball. Roll or pat the dough to a 15-cm / 6-inch square and spread the cherry mixture over the top, leaving a 1 cm / ½ inch border around the edge.

Brush the edge of the dough with milk, then roll it up to enclose the filling. Press the join together. Cut the roll into 8 equal pinwheels and arrange these on top of the gooseberries. Bake for about 15 minutes, until the topping is risen and cooked. Serve at once.

SERVES FOUR

SPICED RHUBARB COBBLER

*Scones flavoured with spices and dried fruit make
a hearty topping for tart stewed rhubarb.*

**675 g / 1½ lb rhubarb, trimmed and sliced
100 g / 4 oz sugar**

**TOPPING
175 g / 6 oz self-raising flour
5 ml / 1 tsp baking powder
40 g / 1½ oz butter or margarine
30 ml / 2 tbsp sugar
5 ml / 1 tsp ground mixed spice
50 g / 2 oz mixed dried fruit
grated rind of 1 orange (optional)
about 75 ml / 3 fl oz milk, plus extra for brushing**

Place the rhubarb and sugar in a heavy-bottomed saucepan and cook gently until the juice begins to run from the fruit and the sugar dissolves. Stirring occasionally, continue to cook the rhubarb gently for 15–20 minutes, until tender. Transfer to an ovenproof dish.

Set the oven at 230°C / 450°F / gas 8. Make the topping. Sift the flour into a bowl with the baking powder. Rub in the butter or margarine until the mixture resembles fine breadcrumbs, then stir in the sugar, spice, dried fruit and orange rind (if used). Mix in enough of the milk to make a soft dough.

Turn the dough out on to a lightly floured surface, knead it gently into a ball and roll it out to about 1 cm / ½ inch thick. Use a 5-cm / 2-inch round cutter to cut out scones. Arrange the scones on top of the fruit.

Brush the scones with milk and bake for 12–15 minutes, until risen and golden.

SERVES FOUR

UPSIDE-DOWN COBBLER

*Take the scone topping that makes a traditional cobbler
and use it as the base for a fruity topping.*

225 g / 8 oz self-raising flour
5 ml / 1 tsp baking powder
50 g / 2 oz butter or margarine
25 g / 1 oz sugar
about 125 ml / 4 fl oz milk
2 cooking apples
50 g / 2 oz black grapes, halved and seeded
1 x 227 g / 8 oz can peach slices, drained
30 ml / 2 tbsp liquid honey
15 ml / 1 tbsp orange juice
25 g / 1 oz flaked almonds

Grease a large baking sheet. Set the oven at 220°C / 425°F / gas 7. Sift the flour
and baking powder into a mixing bowl. Rub in the butter or margarine until the
mixture resembles fine breadcrumbs. Stir in the sugar, then mix in enough milk
to make a soft dough.

Turn the dough out on to a lightly floured surface and knead it very gently into
a smooth ball. Roll or pat out the dough to a 25-cm / 10-inch circle, then lift it
on to the baking sheet.

Peel and core the apples. Slice them into rings and arrange them, overlapping,
around the outer edge of the scone base. Arrange the grapes in a circle inside
the ring of apple slices. Arrange the peach slices in the middle.

Stir the honey and orange juice together in a cup, then brush a little over the
apples; reserve most of the honey and orange juice glaze. Sprinkle the apples
with the flaked almonds and bake for about 15–20 minutes, until the base is
risen and cooked and the nuts on top are lightly browned. Remove the cobbler
from the oven and brush the apples with the reserved glaze. Serve at once.

SERVES SIX TO EIGHT

NUTTY PLUM CRUMBLE

*Tangy plums and toasted hazelnuts make a tasty combination
in this tempting pudding. Apples, rhubarb, gooseberries,
or a mixture of fruit may be used instead of the plums.*

675 g / 1½ lb, plums, halved and stoned
50 g / 2 oz sugar

TOPPING
175 g / 6 oz plain flour
75 g / 3 oz butter or margarine
25 g / 1 oz demerara sugar
5 ml / 1 tsp ground cinnamon
75 g / 3 oz hazelnuts, toasted and chopped

Set the oven at 180°C / 350°F / gas 4. Place the plums in an ovenproof dish and sprinkle with the sugar.

Make the topping. Sift the flour into a mixing bowl and rub in the butter or margarine until the mixture resembles fine breadcrumbs. Stir in the sugar, cinnamon and hazelnuts.

Sprinkle the topping evenly over the plums, pressing it down very lightly. Bake the crumble for about 45 minutes, until the topping is golden brown and the plums are cooked. Serve with custard, cream or Vanilla Ice Cream (page 37).

SERVES FOUR TO SIX

APPLE CRUMBLE

butter for greasing
675 g / 1½ lb cooking apples
100 g / 4 oz granulated sugar
grated rind of 1 lemon
150 g / 5 oz plain flour
75 g / 3 oz butter or margarine
75 g / 3 oz caster sugar
1.25 ml / ¼ tsp ground ginger

Grease a 1-litre / 1¾-pint pie dish. Set the oven at 180°C / 350°F / gas 4. Peel and core the apples. Slice into a saucepan and add the granulated sugar and lemon rind. Stir in 50 ml / 2 fl oz water, cover the pan and cook until the apples are soft. Spoon the apple mixture into the prepared dish and set aside.

Put the flour into a mixing bowl and rub in the butter or margarine until the mixture resembles fine breadcrumbs. Add the caster sugar and ginger and stir well. Sprinkle the mixture over the apples and press down lightly. Bake for 30–40 minutes until the crumble topping is golden brown.

SERVES SIX

VARIATIONS

- Instead of apples, use 675 g / 1½ lb damsons, gooseberries, pears, plums, rhubarb or raspberries.

MICROWAVE TIP

Put the apple mixture in a large bowl, adding only 30 ml / 2 tbsp water, cover and cook for 7 minutes on High. Add the crumble topping and cook for 4 minutes more, then brown the topping under a preheated grill.

BAKED APPLES

**6 cooking apples
75 g / 3 oz sultanas, chopped
50 g / 2 oz demerara sugar**

Wash and core the apples. Cut around the skin of each apple with the tip of a sharp knife two-thirds of the way up from the base. Put the apples into an oven-proof dish, and fill the centres with the chopped sultanas.

Sprinkle the demerara sugar on top of the apples and pour 75 ml / 5 tbsp water around them. Bake for 45–60 minutes, depending on the cooking quality and size of the apples.

Serve accompanied by a vanilla custard, Vanilla Ice Cream (page 37), Brandy Butter (page 237) or with whipped cream.

SERVES SIX

VARIATIONS

- Fill the apple cavities with a mixture of 50 g / 2 oz Barbados or other raw sugar and 50 g / 2 oz butter, or use blackcurrant, raspberry, strawberry or apricot jam, or marmalade. Instead of sultanas, chopped stoned dates, raisins or currants could be used. A topping of toasted almonds looks effective and tastes delicious.

MICROWAVE TIP

Baked apples cook superbly in the microwave. Prepare as suggested above, but reduce the amount of water to 30 ml / 2 tsp. Cook for 10–12 minutes on High.

BAKED APPLES STUFFED WITH RICE AND NUTS

6 medium cooking apples
25 g / 1 oz flaked almonds or other nuts
40 g / 1½ oz seedless raisins
25–50 g / 1–2 oz boiled rice (preferably boiled in milk)
50 g / 2 oz sugar or to taste
1 egg, beaten
30 ml / 2 tbsp butter
raspberry or blackcurrant syrup

Set the oven at 190°C / 375°F / gas 5. Wash and core the apples but do not peel them. With a small rounded spoon, hollow out part of the flesh surrounding the core hole. Do not break the outside skin.

In a bowl, mix together the nuts, raisins and rice, using enough rice to make a stuffing for all the apples. Add the sugar, with enough egg to bind the mixture. Melt the butter and stir it into the mixture.

Fill the apples with the rice mixture. Place in a roasting tin and add hot water to a depth of 5 mm / ¼ inch. Bake for 40 minutes or until the apples are tender. Remove the roasting tin from the oven and transfer the apples to a warmed serving platter, using a slotted spoon. Warm the fruit syrup and pour it over the apples.

SERVES SIX

MICROWAVE TIP

*The rice may be cooked in the microwave.
Place 50 g / 2 oz pudding rice in a large bowl with
30 ml / 2 tbsp sugar. Stir in 600 ml / 1 pint water,
cover and cook on High for 25 minutes. Stir well,
then stir in 300 ml / ½ pint top-of-the-milk or single
cream. Use 25–50 g / 1–2 oz of the cooked rice for
the above pudding and reserve the remainder.*

EVE'S PUDDING

butter for greasing
450 g / 1 lb cooking apples
grated rind and juice of 1 lemon
75 g / 3 oz demerara sugar
75 g / 3 oz butter or margarine
75 g / 3 oz caster sugar
1 egg, beaten
100 g / 4 oz self-raising flour

Grease a 1-litre / 1¾-pint pie dish. Set the oven at 180°C / 350°F / gas 4. Peel and core the apples and slice them thinly into a large bowl. Add the lemon rind and juice, with the demerara sugar. Stir in 15 ml / 1 tbsp water, then tip the mixture into the prepared pie dish.

In a mixing bowl, cream the butter or margarine with the caster sugar until light and fluffy. Beat in the egg. Fold in the flour lightly and spread the mixture over the apples.

Bake for 40–45 minutes until the apples are soft and the sponge is firm. Serve with melted apple jelly and single cream or Greek yogurt.

SERVES FOUR

VARIATIONS

* Instead of apples, use 450 g / 1 lb, apricots, peaches, gooseberries, rhubarb, raspberries or plums.

APPLE CHARLOTTE

butter for greasing
400 g / 14 oz cooking apples
grated rind and juice of 1 lemon
100 g / 4 oz soft light brown sugar
pinch of ground cinnamon
50-75 g / 2–3 oz butter
8–10 large slices of white bread, about 5 mm / 1 inch thick
15 ml / 1 tbsp caster sugar

Generously grease a 1-litre / 1¾-pint charlotte mould or 15-cm / 6-inch cake tin with butter. Set the oven at 180°C / 350°F / gas 4. Peel and core the apples. Slice them into a saucepan and add the lemon rind and juice. Stir in the brown sugar and cinnamon and simmer until the apples soften to a thick purée. Leave to cool.

Melt the butter in a saucepan, then pour into a shallow dish. Cut the crusts off the bread, and dip 1 slice in the butter. Cut it into a round to fit the bottom of the mould or tin. Fill any spaces with extra butter-soaked bread, if necessary. Dip the remaining bread slices in the butter. Use 6 slices to line the inside of the mould. The slices should touch one another to make a bread case.

Fill the bread case with the cooled apple purée. Complete the case by fitting the top with more bread slices. Cover loosely with greased greaseproof paper or foil, and bake for 40–45 minutes. To serve the charlotte turn out and dredge with caster sugar. Serve with bramble jelly and cream.

SERVES FIVE TO SIX

MRS BEETON'S TIP

The mould or tin may be lined with slices of bread and butter, placed buttered side out.

BROWN BETTY

butter for greasing
1 kg / 2¼ lb cooking apples
150 g / 5 oz dried wholewheat breadcrumbs
grated rind and juice of 1 lemon
60 ml / 4 tbsp golden syrup
100 g / 4 oz demerara sugar

Grease a 1-litre / 1¾-pint pie dish. Set the oven at 160°C / 325°F / gas 3.

Peel and core the apples. Slice them thinly into a bowl. Coat the prepared pie dish with a thin layer of breadcrumbs, then fill with alternate layers of apples, lemon rind and breadcrumbs. Put the syrup, sugar and lemon juice into a saucepan. Add 30 ml / 2 tbsp water. Heat until the syrup has dissolved, then pour the mixture over the layered pudding. Bake for 1–1¼ hours until the pudding is brown and the apple cooked. Serve with single cream or custard.

SERVES SIX

MRS BEETON'S TIP

Use a tablespoon dipped in boiling water to measure the golden syrup. The syrup will slide off easily.

FRIAR'S OMELETTE

butter for greasing
1 kg / 2¼ lb cooking apples
grated rind and juice of 1 lemon
75 g / 3 oz butter
100 g / 4 oz sugar
2 eggs, beaten
100 g / 4 oz dried white breadcrumbs

Grease a 1-litre / 1¾-pint pie dish. Set the oven at 220°C / 425°F / gas 7.

Peel and core the apples. Slice them into a saucepan and add the lemon rind and juice, 50 g / 2 oz of the butter, and sugar. Cover the pan and cook the apples until very soft. Remove the pan from the heat and cool slightly.

Stir the eggs into the apple mixture and beat well. Put half the breadcrumbs into the prepared pie dish, cover with the apple mixture, and sprinkle with the remaining breadcrumbs. Dot with the remaining butter and bake for 20–25 minutes. Serve with a vanilla custard.

SERVES FOUR TO FIVE

APPLE MERINGUE

500 ml / 17 fl oz thick apple purée
15 ml / 1 tbsp lemon juice
3 eggs, separated
about 250 g / 9 oz caster sugar

DECORATION
glacé cherries
angelica

Set the oven at 180°C / 350°F / gas 4. Put the apple purée in a bowl and beat in the lemon juice and egg yolks with about 75 g / 3 oz of the sugar. Spoon into a 750-ml / 1¼-pint baking dish, cover, and bake for 15 minutes.

In a clean, grease-free bowl, whisk the egg whites to stiff peaks. Gradually whisk in 150 g / 5 oz of the remaining sugar, adding 15 ml / 1 tbsp at a time. Pile the meringue on top of the apple mixture and sprinkle with the remaining sugar. Return to the oven and bake for a further 15 minutes or until the meringue is pale golden brown in colour. Serve at once with a vanilla custard or single cream.

SERVES FOUR

CHERRY PUDDING

butter for greasing
450 g / 1 lb cherries
75 g / 3 oz soft light brown sugar
50 g / 2 oz cornflour
375 ml / 13 fl oz milk
50 g / 2 oz caster sugar
3 eggs, separated
grated rind of 1 lemon
1.25 ml / ¼ tsp ground cinnamon

Grease a 1 litre / 1¾ pint ovenproof dish. Set the oven at 190°C / 375°F / gas 5. Stone the cherries and put them into a saucepan. Add 600 ml / 4 tbsp water and stir in the brown sugar. Stew very gently until the fruit is just soft. Leave to cool.

In a bowl, mix the cornflour to a paste with a little of the milk. Bring the rest of the milk to the boil in a saucepan, then pour it on to the cornflour mixture. Mix well. Return the mixture to the clean pan and bring to the boil, stirring vigorously all the time to make a very thick sauce. Simmer for 2–3 minutes. Stir in the caster sugar, remove from the heat and leave to cool.

Beat the egg yolks, lemon rind and cinnamon into the cornflour sauce. In a clean, grease-free bowl, whisk the egg whites until stiff but not dry, then fold them into the sauce.

Arrange the cherries in the base of the prepared dish, then top with the sauce mixture. Bake for 35–45 minutes or until risen, just set and golden. Serve at once with single cream.

SERVES FIVE TO SIX

MRS BEETON'S TIP

*A cherry stoner makes short work
of preparing the fruit.*

BAKED SPONGE PUDDING

butter for greasing
100 g / 4 oz butter or margarine
100 g / 4 oz caster sugar
2 eggs, beaten
150 g / 5 oz plain flour
5 ml / 1 tsp baking powder
1.25 ml / ¼ tsp vanilla essence
about 30 ml / 2 tbsp milk

Grease a 1-litre / 1¾-pint pie dish. Set the oven at 180°C / 350°F / gas 4. In a mixing bowl, cream the butter or margarine with the sugar until light and fluffy. Gradually beat in the eggs. Sift the flour and baking powder together into a bowl, then fold them into the creamed mixture. Add the essence and enough milk to form a soft dropping consistency.

Spoon the mixture into the prepared pie dish and bake for 30–35 minutes until well risen and golden brown.

Serve from the dish with a vanilla custard or any sweet sauce.

SERVES FOUR TO SIX

VARIATIONS

- **Jam Sponge** Put 30 ml / 2 tbsp jam in the base of the dish before adding the sponge mixture. Serve with a jam sauce made with the same type of jam.
- **Orange or Lemon Sponge** Add the grated rind of 1 orange or 1 lemon to the creamed mixture. Serve the pudding with Rich Lemon Sauce (page 216).
- **Spicy Sponge** Sift 5 ml / 1 tsp mixed spice, ground ginger, grated nutmeg or cinnamon with the flour. Serve with Ginger Syrup Sauce (page 235).
- **Coconut Sponge** Substitute 25 g / 1 oz desiccated coconut for 25 g / 1 oz flour. Serve with Apricot Sauce (page 228).
- **Chocolate Sponge** Substitute 50 g / 2 oz cocoa for 50 g / 2 oz flour. Serve with Chocolate Cream Sauce (page 231) or Chocolate Liqueur Sauce (page 232).

CASTLE PUDDINGS

butter for greasing
100 g / 4 oz butter or margarine
100 g / 4 oz caster sugar
2 eggs
1.25 ml / ¼ tsp vanilla essence
100 g / 4 oz plain flour
5 ml / 1 tsp baking powder

Grease 6–8 dariole moulds. Set the oven at 180°C / 350°F / gas 4.

In a mixing bowl, cream the butter or margarine with the sugar until light and creamy. Beat in the eggs and vanilla essence. Sift the flour and baking powder into a bowl, then fold into the creamed mixture.

Three-quarters fill the prepared dariole moulds. Bake for 20–25 minutes, until set and well risen. Serve with a vanilla custard or Jam Sauce (page 236).

SERVES THREE TO FOUR

VARIATION

- **Somerset Puddings** Let the puddings cool, scoop out the centres and fill the cavity with stewed apple or jam. Serve with whipped cream.

ALMOND CASTLES

butter for greasing
75 g / 3 oz butter
75 g / 3 oz caster sugar
3 eggs, separated
45 ml / 3 tbsp single cream or milk
15 ml / 1 tbsp brandy
150 g / 5 oz ground almonds

Grease 8 dariole moulds. Set the oven at 160°C / 325°F / gas 3.

In a mixing bowl, cream the butter and sugar until light and fluffy. Stir in the egg yolks, cream or milk, brandy and ground almonds.

In a clean, grease-free bowl, whisk the egg whites until just stiff, and fold lightly into the mixture. Three-quarters fill the dariole moulds and bake for 20–25 minutes, until the puddings are firm in the centre and golden brown.

Turn out on to individual plates and serve with a vanilla custard.

SERVES FOUR TO EIGHT

HONESTY PUDDING

butter for greasing
50 g / 2 oz fine oatmeal
15 ml / 1 tbsp plain flour
750 ml / 1¼ pints milk
1 egg, beaten
pinch of salt
2.5 ml / ½ tsp grated orange rind

Grease a 750-ml / 1¼-pint pie dish. Set the oven at 180°C / 350°F / gas 4. Put the oatmeal and flour in a bowl and mix to a smooth paste with a little of the milk. Bring the rest of the milk to the boil in a saucepan, then pour it over the oatmeal mixture, stirring all the time.

Return the mixture to the clean pan and cook over low heat for 5 minutes, stirring all the time. Remove from the heat, and cool for 5 minutes.

Beat the egg into the cooled oatmeal mixture. Flavour with the salt and orange rind. Pour the mixture into the prepared pie dish, and bake for 35–40 minutes.

Serve hot from the dish, with single cream and brown sugar.

SERVES FOUR

LEMON DELICIOUS PUDDING

This pudding has a light spongy top
with lemon sauce underneath.

butter for greasing
3 eggs, separated
75 g / 3 oz caster sugar
200 ml / 7 fl oz milk
15 ml / 1 tbsp self-raising flour, sifted
grated rind and juice of 2 large lemons
pinch of salt
15 ml / 1 tbsp icing sugar

Grease a deep 1-litre / 1¾-pint ovenproof dish. Set the oven at 180°C / 350°F / gas 4.

In a mixing bowl, beat the egg yolks together with the caster sugar until light, pale and creamy. Whisk the milk, flour, rind and lemon juice into the egg yolks. In a clean, grease-free bowl, whisk the egg whites with the salt, adding the icing sugar gradually. Continue to whisk until stiff but not dry. Fold into the lemon mixture.

Pour the mixture into the prepared dish and stand the dish in a roasting tin. Add hot water to come halfway up the sides of the dish. Bake for 1 hour.

SERVES FOUR

MRS BEETON'S TIP

If a fragment of shell drops into the
egg white, the easiest way to remove
it is to use another piece of shell.

BAKED JAM ROLL

butter for greasing
300 g / 11 oz plain flour
5 ml / 1 tsp baking powder
pinch of salt
150 g / 5 oz shredded suet
flour for rolling out
200–300 g / 7–11 oz jam

Grease a baking sheet. Set the oven at 190°C / 375°F / gas 5.

Sift the flour, baking powder and salt into a mixing bowl. Add the suet and enough cold water to make a soft, but firm dough. On a lightly floured surface, roll the dough out to a rectangle about 5 mm / ¼ inch thick. Spread the jam almost to the edges. Dampen the edges of the pastry rectangle with water and roll up lightly. Seal the edges at either end.

Place the roll on the prepared baking sheet with the sealed edge underneath. Cover loosely with greased greaseproof paper or foil and bake for 50–60 minutes until golden brown. Transfer to a warm platter, slice and serve with warmed jam of the same type as that used in the roll.

SERVES SIX

VARIATION

• Instead of the jam, use 200–300 g / 7–11 oz marmalade, or 225 g / 8 oz dried fruit mixed with 50 g / 2 oz demerara sugar. Serve with a vanilla custard or Rich Lemon Sauce (page 216).

BREAD AND BUTTER PUDDING

When the weather is dull and dreary, lift the spirits
with this comforting old favourite.

butter for greasing
4 thin slices of bread (about 100 g / 4 oz)
25 g / 1 oz butter
50 g / 2 oz sultanas or currants
pinch of ground nutmeg or cinnamon
400 ml / 14 fl oz milk
2 eggs
25 g / 1 oz granulated sugar

Grease a 1-litre / 1¾-pint pie dish. Cut the crusts off the bread and spread the slices with the butter. Cut the bread into squares or triangles and arrange in alternate layers, buttered side up, with the sultanas or currants. Sprinkle each layer lightly with nutmeg or cinnamon. Arrange the top layer of bread in an attractive pattern.

Warm the milk in a saucepan to about 65°C / 150°F. Do not let it approach boiling point. Put the eggs in a bowl. Add most of the sugar. Beat with a fork and stir in the milk. Strain the custard mixture over the bread, sprinkle some nutmeg and the remaining sugar on top, and leave to stand for 30 minutes. Set the oven at 180°C / 350°F / gas 4. Bake for 30–40 minutes until the custard is set and the top is lightly browned.

SERVES FOUR

PRESSURE COOKER TIP

Use a dish that fits in the pressure cooker.
Cover the pudding with foil or greased
greaseproof paper, tied down securely.
Cook at 15 1b pressure for 9 minutes.
Reduce pressure slowly, then brown
the pudding under the grill.

SHAHI TUKRA

An Asian version of bread and butter pudding.

3 medium slices of white bread
2 cardamoms
2 whole unblanched almonds
4 whole unblanched pistachio nuts
40 g / 1½ oz ghee or butter
250 ml / 8 fl oz milk
few strands of saffron
45 ml / 3 tbsp sugar
75 ml / 3 fl oz double cream
30 ml / 2 tbsp single cream
pinch of grated nutmeg

Cut the crusts off the bread. Cut each slice into 4 triangular pieces. Split the cardamom pods, pick out and crush the seeds, discarding the outer husk. Crush the almonds and pistachio nuts with their skins.

Heat the ghee or butter in a frying pan, and fry the bread until golden brown on both sides. Drain on absorbent kitchen paper.

Heat the milk slowly in a shallow saucepan over moderate heat. When it begins to steam, add the saffron strands and sugar. Reduce to very low heat, and cook gently for 20 minutes.

Add the double cream to the saffron mixture and cook for a further 10 minutes. The sauce should be thickened but runny. Drop the fried bread triangles into the sauce. Turn them over after 5 minutes. Cook very slowly until the sauce is absorbed by the fried bread.

Serve hot or cold, covered with the single cream. Top each portion with a generous sprinkling of the crushed nuts and cardamom, adding a pinch of grated nutmeg.

SERVES FOUR TO FIVE

POOR KNIGHTS

'Poor Knights' originated in England in the Middle Ages,
but soon became popular all over Europe.
Every country has its own traditional variation,
with more elaborate versions called 'Rich Knights'.
Some are made with sweet bread or stale cake,
others are moistened with red wine.

4 thick slices of white bread
2 eggs, beaten
200 ml / 7 fl oz milk or white wine
1.25 ml / ¼ tsp cinnamon
15 ml / 1 tbsp sugar
oil for shallow frying
caster sugar and ground cinnamon to serve

Cut the crusts off the bread, then cut each slice into quarters. Place them in a deep dish.

In a bowl, mix the eggs with the milk or wine, cinnamon and sugar. Pour the liquid over the bread, cover, and leave to soak for 2–3 minutes.

Heat oil to a depth of 5 mm / ¼ inch in a frying pan. Using a palette knife or fish slice, drain a square of bread from the dish. Slide the bread into the hot oil. Add 1 or 2 more squares, drained in the same way. Fry until golden brown on both sides, turning once.

Drain the 'Poor Knights' on absorbent kitchen paper, then keep uncovered in a warm place until needed. Fry the remaining bread squares in the same way. Serve sprinkled with caster sugar and cinnamon.

SERVES FOUR

SALZBURGER NOCKERL

50 g / 2 oz butter
10 ml / 2 tsp caster sugar
5 eggs, separated
15 ml / 1 tbsp plain flour
125 ml / 4 fl oz milk
icing sugar for dredging

Set the oven at 200°C / 400°F / gas 6. Beat the butter and sugar together in a mixing bowl until light and fluffy. Stir in the egg yolks one at a time.

In a clean, grease-free bowl, whisk the egg whites until stiff, and fold lightly into the egg yolk mixture with the flour.

Pour the milk into a shallow flameproof dish, and heat gently. Remove from the heat, pour in the batter, smooth it lightly, and bake for about 10 minutes until light brown in colour. Cut out spoonfuls of the nockerl, and arrange on a warmed serving plate. Serve immediately, sprinkled with icing sugar.

SERVES FOUR TO SIX

BUTTERSCOTCH PUDDING

25 g / 1 oz cornflour
500 ml / 17 fl oz milk
2 eggs, separated
100 g / 4 oz soft light brown sugar
25 g / 1 oz butter
5 ml / 1 tsp vanilla essence
25 g / 1 oz walnuts, chopped, to decorate

In a bowl, mix the cornflour to a paste with a little of the cold milk. Bring the rest of the milk to the boil in a saucepan, and pour on to the blended cornflour, stirring to prevent the formation of lumps.

Return the mixture to the clean pan and bring to simmering point, stirring all the time. Simmer for 2–3 minutes. Cool for 3–4 minutes.

Add the egg yolks to the pan. Stir thoroughly, and cook without boiling for a further 2–3 minutes.

Melt the sugar in a heavy-bottomed saucepan and add the butter. When the butter has melted, stir the mixture into the cornflour sauce.

In a clean, grease-free bowl whisk the egg whites until fairly stiff and fold lightly into the pudding mixture. Add the essence. Pile into a serving dish and refrigerate for about 1 hour to set. Sprinkle the dessert with the walnuts before serving.

SERVES SIX

RUM BABAS

oil for greasing
75 ml / 5 tbsp milk
10 ml / 2 tsp dried yeast
150 g / 5 oz strong white flour
1.25 ml / ¼ tsp salt
10 ml / 2 tsp caster sugar
75 g / 3 oz butter
3 eggs, beaten
50 g / 2 oz currants

RUM SYRUP
75 g / 3 oz lump sugar
30 ml / 2 tbsp rum
15 ml / 1 tbsp lemon juice

Oil 12 baba tins. Set the oven at 200°C / 400°F / gas 6. Warm the milk until tepid. Sprinkle on the dried yeast. Stir in 15 ml / 1 tbsp of the flour and leave in a warm place for 20 minutes.

Sift the rest of the flour, the salt and the sugar into a mixing bowl. Rub in the butter. Add the yeast liquid to the mixture, then add the eggs. Beat until well mixed, then work in the currants. Half fill the prepared tins with mixture. Cover with oiled polythene, and leave in a warm place until the tins are two-thirds full. Bake for 10–15 minutes or until the babas are golden brown and spongy to the touch.

Heat the lump sugar in a saucepan with 125 ml / 4 fl oz water. Stir until the sugar has dissolved, then boil the mixture steadily for 6–8 minutes, without stirring, until it forms a syrup. Stir in the rum and lemon juice.

Remove the babas from the tins, prick all over with a fine skewer and transfer to individual dishes. Spoon hot rum syrup over each baba. Serve cold, with cream.

SERVES TWELVE

RING OF PEARS

butter for greasing
3 slices of plain cake or trifle sponges
400 ml / 14 fl oz milk
25 g / 1 oz butter
2 eggs
1 egg yolk
25 g / 1 oz caster sugar
5 ml / 1 tsp grated lemon rind
1 x 425 g / 15 oz can pear halves in syrup
red food colouring (optional)

Grease a 600-ml / 1-pint ring mould. Cut the cake vertically into 1-cm / ½-inch slices and arrange these in the mould. Set the oven at 150°C / 300°F / gas 2.

Warm the milk and butter in a saucepan until the butter just melts. In a bowl, mix together the whole eggs and yolk, the sugar and grated lemon rind. Stir in the warmed milk mixture and strain the mixture over the cake slices. Cover with greased greaseproof paper or foil.

Stand the pudding in a roasting tin. Add hot water to come halfway up the sides of the ring mould and bake for about 1 hour or until set.

Meanwhile drain the pears, reserving the fruit and boiling the syrup in a saucepan until slightly reduced. Add a few drops of red food colouring, if the fruit is very pale.

Leave the cooked pudding to stand for a few minutes, then carefully unmould the ring on to a warmed dish. Arrange the reserved pears in the centre, pouring the syrup over them. Serve at once.

SERVES FOUR

VARIATION

- Use apricots or peaches instead of pears.

QUEEN OF PUDDINGS

butter for greasing
75 g / 3 oz fresh white breadcrumbs
400 ml / 14 fl oz milk
25 g / 1 oz butter
10 ml / 2 tsp grated lemon rind
2 eggs, separated
75 g / 3 oz caster sugar
30 ml / 2 tbsp red jam

Grease a 750-ml / 1¼-pint pie dish. Set the oven at 160°C / 325°F / gas 3. Spread the breadcrumbs out on a baking sheet and put into the oven to dry off slightly.

Warm the milk and butter with the lemon rind in a saucepan. Meanwhile put the egg yolks in a bowl and stir in 25 g / 1 oz of the sugar. Pour on the warmed milk mixture, stirring thoroughly. Add the breadcrumbs, mix thoroughly and pour into the prepared pie dish. Leave to stand for 30 minutes.

Bake the pudding for 40–50 minutes until lightly set, then remove from the oven. Lower the oven temperature to 120°C / 250°F / gas 1. Warm the jam in a small saucepan until runny, then spread it over the top of the pudding.

In a clean, grease-free bowl, whisk the egg whites until stiff. Add half the remaining sugar and whisk again. Fold in all but 15 ml / 1 tbsp of the remaining sugar. Spoon the meringue around the edge of the jam, drawing it up into peaks at regular intervals to resemble a crown. Sprinkle with the rest of the sugar.

Return the pudding to the oven and bake for 40–45 minutes more, until the meringue is set.

SERVES FOUR

MICROWAVE TIP
Warm the jam for a
few seconds on High.

CUSTARD TART

250 ml / 8 fl oz milk
2 eggs
50 g / 2 oz caster sugar
pinch of grated nutmeg

SHORT CRUST PASTRY
100 g / 4 oz plain flour
1.25 ml / ¼ tsp salt
50 g / 2 oz margarine (or half butter, half lard)
flour for rolling out

Put an 18-cm / 7-inch flan ring on a heavy baking sheet. Alternatively, line an 18-cm / 7-inch sandwich cake tin with foil. Set the oven at 190°C / 375°F / gas 5.

Make the pastry. Sift the flour and salt into a bowl, then rub in the margarine until the mixture resembles fine breadcrumbs. Add enough cold water to make a stiff dough. Press the dough together with your fingertips. Roll out on a lightly floured surface and use to line the flan ring or tin.

In a saucepan, bring the milk to just below boiling point. Put the eggs and caster sugar into a bowl, mix well, then stir in the scalded milk. Strain the mixture into the pastry case and sprinkle the top with grated nutmeg. Bake for 10 minutes.

Lower the oven temperature to 150°C / 300°F / gas 2 and bake for 15–20 minutes more or until the custard is just set. Serve hot or cold.

SERVES FOUR TO SIX

Sauces

A well-chosen, perfectly prepared sauce adds a professional touch to a dessert. Custard, cream, caramel, chocolate, alcohol, fruit, or a melting, flavoured butter, these recipes will turn any pudding into a treat.

PREPARING YOUR DESSERT SAUCE

When serving a cold sauce, prepare it in advance, cool and chill it until it is needed. If you are preparing a hot sauce that requires last-minute attention weigh all the ingredients and set out all the utensils beforehand. Some hot sauces may be made and put on one side ready for last-minute reheating. To prevent the formation of a skin on a sauce, cover it with a piece of dampened greaseproof paper; alternatively, sprinkle a little caster sugar over the surface.

REDCURRANT SAUCE

100 g / 4 oz redcurrant jelly
45 ml / 3 tbsp port

Combine the jelly and port in a small saucepan and cook over gentle heat until the jelly melts. Pour over steamed puddings or serve with hot milk puddings such as semolina. The sauce also makes a good glaze for cheesecakes topped with berry fruits.

MAKES ABOUT 150 ml / ¼ pint

APPLE AND ORANGE SAUCE

Rich and full of flavour, this is an ideal accompaniment to steamed fruit puddings. Cold, it makes a good filling for apple meringue pie or cake.

450 g / 1 lb cooking apples
15 g / 1 oz butter or margarine
finely grated rind and juice of 1 orange
sugar (see method)

Peel and core the apples and slice them into a saucepan. Add 30 ml / 2 tbsp water with the butter and orange rind. Cover the pan and cook over low heat until the apple is reduced to a pulp.

Beat the pulp until smooth, then rub through a sieve. Alternatively, purée the mixture in a blender or food processor.

Return the purée to the clean pan and reheat. Stir in the orange juice, with sugar to taste. Serve hot or cold.

MAKES 375 ml / 13 fl oz

MICROWAVE TIP

Place the sliced apples in a large dish or bowl with the water, butter and orange rind. Make sure there is room for the apples to boil up. Cover and cook on High for 5-7 minutes, stirring once. Continue as above.

SWEET ARROWROOT SAUCE

The advantage in using arrowroot is that it creates a clear
sauce that will not mask the pudding over which it is poured.
A thinner sauce may be made by increasing the water
in the saucepan to 250 ml / 8 fl oz.

thinly pared rind of 1 lemon or
other solid flavouring
100 g / 4 oz sugar
lemon juice
10 ml / 2 tsp arrowroot

Put 125 ml / 4 fl oz water in a saucepan. Add the lemon rind or other flavouring and bring to the boil. Lower the heat and simmer the sauce gently for 15 minutes.

Remove the lemon rind, if used, and stir in the sugar. Return the liquid to the boil and boil steadily for 5 minutes. Stir in lemon juice to taste.

In a cup, mix the arrowroot with 15 ml / 2 tsp water until smooth. Stir into the hot liquid. Heat gently for 1–2 minutes, stirring constantly as the sauce thickens. Remove from the heat once the sauce has boiled.

MAKES ABOUT 175 ml / 6 fl oz

VARIATIONS

- **St Clement's Sauce** Use the rind of ½ lemon or ½ orange and add 125 ml / 4 fl oz lemon or orange juice.
- **Rich Lemon Sauce** Beat 125 ml / 4 fl oz sherry with 1 egg yolk. Add the mixture to the thickened sauce and heat gently. Do not allow the sauce to boil once the egg yolk mixture has been added.

SWEET WHITE SAUCE

20 ml / 4 tsp cornflour
250 ml / 8 fl oz milk
15–30 ml / 1–2 tbsp sugar
vanilla essence or other flavouring

Put the cornflour in a bowl. Stir in enough of the cold milk to form a smooth, thin paste.

Heat the remaining milk in a small saucepan. When it boils, stir it into the cornflour paste, then return the mixture to the clean pan and stir until boiling.

Lower the heat and cook, stirring frequently, for 3 minutes. Stir in sugar to taste and add the chosen flavouring. Serve hot.

MAKES ABOUT 250 ml / 8 fl oz

VARIATIONS

- **Almond Sauce** Add 10 ml / 2 tsp ground almonds to the cornflour when blending with the milk. When the sauce is cooked, stir in 2–3 drops of almond essence with vanilla essence to taste.
- **Brandy Sauce** When the sauce is cooked, stir in 15–30 ml / 1–2 tbsp brandy.
- **Chocolate Sauce** When the sauce is cooked, stir in 15 ml / 1 tbsp cocoa dissolved in 15 ml / 1 tbsp boiling water.
- **Coffee Sauce** To the cooked sauce add 10 ml / 2 tsp instant coffee dissolved in 15 ml / 1 tbsp boiling water.
- **Ginger Sauce** Stir in 10 ml / 2 tsp ground ginger with the cornflour. For extra taste and texture, 50 g / 2 oz crystallized ginger, finely chopped, may be added to the cooked sauce.

VANILLA CUSTARD

*Adding cornflour stabilizes the custard
and makes it less inclined to curdle.*

10 ml / 2 tsp cornflour
500 ml / 17 fl oz milk
25 g / 1 oz caster sugar
2 eggs
vanilla essence

In a bowl, mix the cornflour to a smooth paste with a little of the cold milk. Heat the rest of the milk in a saucepan and when hot pour it on to the blended cornflour, stirring.

Return to the mixture to the pan, bring to the boil and boil for 1–2 minutes, stirring all the time, to cook the cornflour. Remove from the heat and stir in the sugar. Leave to cool.

Beat the eggs together lightly in a small bowl. Add a little of the cooked cornflour mixture, stir well, then pour into the pan. Heat gently for a few minutes until the custard has thickened, stirring all the time. Do not boil. Stir in a few drops of vanilla essence.

Serve hot or cold as an accompaniment to a pudding or pie.

MAKES ABOUT 600 ml / 1 pint

SIMPLE CUSTARD SAUCE

The addition of cornflour makes it unnecessary
to use a double saucepan to make this sauce,
provided care is taken to avoid excessive heat
and the custard is constantly stirred.

500 ml / 17 fl oz milk
few drops of vanilla essence
6 egg yolks
100 g / 4 oz caster sugar
10 ml / 2 tsp cornflour

Combine the milk and vanilla essence in a saucepan. Warm gently but do not allow to boil.

In a bowl, beat the egg yolks, sugar and cornflour together until creamy. Add the warm milk.

Strain the mixture back into the clean pan and cook, stirring constantly, until the custard thickens and coats the back of the spoon. Serve hot or cold.

MAKES ABOUT 600 ml / 1 pint

CORNFLOUR CUSTARD SAUCE

15 ml / 1 tbsp cornflour
250ml / 8 fl oz milk
1 egg yolk
15 ml / 1 tbsp sugar
few drops of vanilla essence

Mix the cornflour with a little of the cold milk in a large bowl. Bring the rest of the milk to the boil in a saucepan, then stir into the blended mixture. Return the mixture to the clean pan.

Bring the cornflour mixture to the boil and boil for 3 minutes to cook the cornflour. Remove from the heat.

When the mixture has cooled a little, stir in the egg yolk and sugar. Return to low heat and cook, stirring carefully, until the sauce thickens. Do not let it boil. Flavour with a few drops of vanilla essence and pour into a jug.

MAKES ABOUT 250 ml / 8 fl oz

MICROWAVE TIP

Mix the cornflour with all the milk in a bowl. Cook on High for 3–5 minutes, whisking twice. Whisk well, then whisk in the yolk, sugar and vanilla. Cook for a further 30–45 seconds on High.

CARAMEL CUSTARD SAUCE

25 g / 1 oz granulated sugar
250 ml / 8 fl oz milk
few drops of vanilla essence or a strip of lemon rind
3 egg yolks
50 g / 2 oz caster sugar

Start by making the caramel. Mix the granulated sugar with 15 ml / 1 tbsp water in a small saucepan. Heat gently until the sugar dissolves, then boil the syrup until it is golden brown. Remove the syrup from the heat and immediately add 30 ml / 2 tbsp cold water (see Mrs Beeton's Tip). Leave in a warm place to dissolve.

Meanwhile, make the sauce. Combine the milk and chosen flavouring in a saucepan. Warm gently but do not let the liquid boil.

In a bowl, beat the egg yolks and sugar together until creamy. Remove the lemon rind, if used, from the pan and add the milk to the eggs.

Strain the custard into a double saucepan or a heatproof bowl placed over a saucepan of simmering water. Cook, stirring constantly, until the custard thickens and coats the back of the spoon.

Stir the caramel. Add enough to the finished custard sauce to give a good flavour and colour. Serve warm or cold.

MAKES ABOUT 300 ml / ½ PINT

MRS BEETON'S TIP

Take care when adding the cold water to the hot caramel. The mixture may spit, so it is wise to protect your hand by wearing an oven glove.

CLASSIC
EGG CUSTARD SAUCE

*This recipe may be used as the basis for ice cream
or for Vanilla Bavarois (page 92)*

**500 ml / 17 fl oz milk
few drops of vanilla essence or other
flavouring
6 egg yolks
100 g / 4 oz caster sugar**

Put the milk in a saucepan with the vanilla or other flavouring. Warm gently but do not let the liquid boil. If a solid flavouring such as a strip of citrus rind is used, allow it to infuse in the milk for 5 minutes, then remove.

In a bowl, beat the egg yolks and sugar together until creamy. Add the warm milk to the egg mixture.

Strain the mixture into a double saucepan or a heatproof bowl placed over a saucepan of simmering water. Cook, stirring constantly with a wooden spoon for 20–30 minutes, until the custard thickens and coats the back of the spoon. Take care not to let the custard curdle. Serve hot or cold.

MAKES ABOUT 500 ml / 17 fl oz

VARIATIONS

- **Classic Lemon Custard** Infuse a thin strip of lemon rind in the milk, removing it before adding to the eggs.
- **Classic Orange Custard** Substitute orange for lemon rind.
- **Classic Liqueur Custard** Add 15 ml / 1 tbsp kirsch or curaçao at the end of the cooking time.
- **Praline Custard** Stir in crushed praline (see Mrs Beeton's Tip, page 73) just before serving the custard.

CRÈME ANGLAISE

The classic egg custard sauce; and an
essential ingredient of many desserts.

250 ml / 8 fl oz milk
few drops of vanilla essence or a strip of lemon rind
3 egg yolks
50 g / 2 oz caster sugar

Combine the milk and chosen flavouring in a saucepan. Warm gently but do not allow to boil.

In a bowl, beat the egg yolks and sugar together until creamy. Remove the lemon rind, if used, from the saucepan and add the milk to the eggs.

Strain the custard into a double saucepan or a heatproof bowl placed over a saucepan of simmering water. Cook, stirring constantly, until the custard thickens and coats the back of the spoon. Serve hot or cold.

MAKES 300 ml / ½ PINT

VARIATIONS

* **Liqueur Sauce** Stir 125 ml / 4 fl oz lightly whipped double cream and 30 ml / 2 tbsp orange-flavoured liqueur into the sauce.
* **Chocolate Custard Sauce** Use vanilla essence instead of lemon rind and add 100 g / 4 oz coarsely grated plain chocolate to the milk. Warm until the chocolate melts, stir, then add to the egg yolks and proceed as in the main recipe.

CREAM CUSTARD SAUCE

4 egg yolks or 2 whole eggs
50 g / 2 oz caster sugar
125 ml / 4 fl oz milk
grated rind of 1 orange
125 ml / 4 fl oz single cream

In a mixing bowl, beat the egg yolks or the whole eggs with the sugar and milk. Stir in the orange rind and cream.

Pour into a double saucepan or into a heatproof bowl placed over a saucepan of simmering water. Cook, stirring all the time, until the sauce thickens. Serve hot or cold.

MAKES ABOUT 250 ml / 8 fl oz

MRS BEETON'S TIP

*Do not allow the sauce to
boil or it will curdle.*

CHANTILLY CREAM

250 ml / 8 fl oz double cream
25 g / 1 oz icing sugar
few drops of vanilla essence

Pour the cream into a mixing bowl and chill it for several hours.

Just before serving, whip the cream with the sugar and vanilla essence to taste.

MAKES ABOUT 250 ml / 8 fl oz

PLUM PUDDING SAUCE

*A thin sauce with a rich, buttery flavour to make a potent impression
on Christmas pudding or a variety of other desserts.*

100 g / 4 oz caster sugar
75 ml / 3 fl oz brandy
50 g / 2 oz unsalted butter, diced
175 ml / 6 fl oz Madeira

Put the sugar in a heatproof bowl with 30 ml / 2 tbsp of the brandy. Add the
butter. Set over simmering water and stir until the mixture is smooth. Gradually
stir in the rest of the brandy with the Madeira and warm through. Either serve
over the pudding or in a sauceboat.

MAKES 350 ml / 12 fl oz

CARAMEL

200 g / 7 oz caster sugar

Put the sugar in a heavy-bottomed saucepan. Add 125 ml / 4 fl oz water and stir
over low heat for 3–4 minutes until the sugar has dissolved. Increase the heat
and boil, without stirring, until the syrup is a light golden brown. Do not allow
it to darken too much or it will taste bitter.

Immediately plunge the bottom of the pan into warm water to prevent further
cooking. Allow the caramel mixture to cool slightly, then carefully add a
further 75 ml / 3 fl oz water. Return the pan to a low heat and stir constantly
until the mixture becomes smooth. Remove from the heat, cool slightly, then
use as required.

SERVES FOUR

SABAYON SAUCE

The French version of that Italian favourite,
Zabaglione, Sabayon is usually served warm
as an accompaniment to steamed pudding.

3 egg yolks
25 g / 1 oz caster sugar
50 ml / 2 fl oz Marsala, Madeira, sweet sherry or
sweet white wine
small strip of lemon rind

Beat the yolks and sugar together in a heatproof bowl until thick and pale. Gradually whisk in the chosen wine. Add the lemon rind.

Pour the mixture into a double saucepan or stand the bowl over a saucepan of simmering water. Cook until thick and creamy, whisking all the time. When the whisk is lifted out of the mixture it should leave a trail that lasts for 2–3 seconds. Remove the lemon rind and serve at once.

MAKES ABOUT 200 ml / 7 fl oz

MICROWAVE TIP

Whisk the yolks and sugar as above,
in a bowl which may be used in the
microwave. In a jug, heat the chosen
wine on High for 30–45 seconds,
until hot but not boiling, then whisk
it into the yolks. Cook on High for
about 1–1½ minutes, whisking
thoroughly two or three times,
until creamy.

COLD SHERRY SABAYON SAUCE

50 g / 2 oz caster sugar
2 egg yolks
15 ml / 1 tbsp medium-sweet sherry or brandy
45 ml / 3 tbsp double cream

Put the sugar in a saucepan with 75 ml / 5 tbsp water. Warm gently until the sugar is completely dissolved, then bring to the boil and boil for 3 minutes.

Mix the egg yolks with the sherry or brandy in a bowl. Whisk in the syrup gradually, and continue whisking until the mixture is cool, thick and foamy. In a second bowl, whip the cream lightly. Fold it gently into the egg mixture. Chill.

Pour into tall glasses and serve with ratafias. The sauce may also be served with cold desserts or fresh fruit.

MAKES ABOUT 400 ml / 14 fl oz

SWEET MOUSSELINE SAUCE

Serve this frothy sauce over light steamed or baked puddings,
fruit desserts or Christmas pudding.

2 whole eggs plus 1 yolk
40 g / 1½ oz caster sugar
75 ml / 5 tbsp single cream
15 ml / 1 tbsp medium-dry sherry

Combine all the ingredients in a double saucepan or in a heatproof bowl placed over a saucepan of simmering water. Cook and whisk until pale and frothy and of a thick, creamy consistency. Pour into a bowl and serve at once.

MAKES ABOUT 300 ml / ½ pint

APRICOT SAUCE

This fruity sauce may be served hot or cold, with set custards, sponge puddings, pancakes or ice cream. It also makes an unusual, lively accompaniment to plain apple pie.

225 g / 8 oz fresh apricots
25–50 g / 1–2 oz soft light brown sugar
15 ml / 1 tbsp lemon juice
10 ml / 2 tsp maraschino or apricot brandy (optional)
5 ml / 1 tsp arrowroot

Stone the apricots, reserving the stones. Put the fruit into a saucepan with 125 ml / 4 fl oz water. Cover the pan and simmer the fruit until softened. Rub through a sieve, or purée in a blender or food processor.

Crack the reserved apricot stones and remove the kernels. Cover the kernels with boiling water and leave for 2 minutes. Drain the kernels, and when cool enough to handle, skin them. Add to the apricots with sugar to taste and stir in the lemon juice with the liqueur, if used. Reheat the sauce.

In a cup, mix the arrowroot with 15 ml / 1 tbsp water. Add to the sauce and bring to the boil, stirring until the sauce thickens. Serve.

MAKES ABOUT 375 ml / 13 fl oz

MRS BEETON'S TIP

If time is short, substitute 1 x 425 g / 15 oz can apricots for fresh fruit. Purée the drained fruit with 125 ml / 4 fl oz of the can syrup. Sugar need not be added, but lemon juice and liqueur, if used, should be added before the sauce is reheated.

THICKENED FRUIT SAUCE

**450 g / 1 lb ripe fruit (damsons, plums,
berry fruits)
50–100 g / 2–4 oz sugar
lemon juice
arrowroot (see method)**

Put the fruit into a saucepan with about 30 ml / 2 tbsp water. Cover the pan and cook over low heat until the fruit is reduced to a pulp. Remove any stones.

Beat the pulp until smooth, then rub through a sieve. Alternatively, purée the mixture in a blender or food processor. Pour the purée into a measuring jug; note the volume.

Return the purée to the clean pan and reheat. Stir in the sugar, with lemon juice to taste. To thicken the sauce, you will need 5 ml / 1 tsp arrowroot for every 250 ml / 8 fl oz fruit purée. Spoon the required amount of arrowroot into a cup or small bowl and mix to a paste with water. Add to the fruit mixture and bring to the boil, stirring constantly until the sauce thickens. Remove from the heat as soon as the sauce boils. Serve hot or cold.

MAKES ABOUT 400 ml / 14 fl oz

FREEZER TIP

*It is best to freeze the fruit purée
before thickening. Pour into a
rigid container, cover and seal.
It will keep for up to 12 months.
When required, thaw for 4 hours,
reheat gently and thicken the sauce
as described above.*

COLD CHANTILLY APPLE SAUCE

450 g / 1 lb cooking apples
25 g / 1 oz butter
50 g / 2 oz sugar
150 ml / 1 pint double cream

Peel, core and slice the apples, Put them into a saucepan with 30 ml / 2 tbsp water. Add the butter and sugar. Cover the pan and simmer gently until the apple is reduced to a pulp.

Beat the pulp until smooth, then rub the mixture through a sieve. Alternatively, purée in a blender or food processor. Pour into a bowl and leave to cool.

In a separate bowl, whip the cream until stiff. Fold gently into the apple purée. Serve cold.

MAKES ABOUT 500 ml / 17 fl oz

FRUIT AND YOGURT SAUCE

Any fruit purée may he used for this sauce,
provided it is not too acidic. Use fresh or canned
fruit – apricots are particularly good.

150 ml / 1 pint plain yogurt
250 ml / 8 fl oz fruit purée
sugar to taste

Spoon the yogurt into a bowl and beat it lightly. Fold in the fruit purée. Add sugar to taste. Serve the sauce cold.

MAKES ABOUT 350 ml / 12 fl oz

CHOCOLATE CREAM SAUCE

Add a touch of luxury to rice pudding, poached pears or ice cream with this sauce. When cold, the sauce thickens enough to be used as a soft filling for éclairs or profiteroles.

75 g / 3 oz plain chocolate, roughly grated
15 ml / 1 tbsp butter
15 ml / 1 tbsp single cream
5 ml / 1 tsp vanilla essence

Put the grated chocolate in a heatproof bowl with the butter. Add 60 ml / 4 tbsp water. Stand the bowl over a saucepan of simmering water and stir until the chocolate and butter have melted.

When the chocolate mixture is smooth, remove from the heat and immediately stir in the cream and vanilla essence. Serve at once.

MAKES ABOUT 125 ml / 4 fl oz

MICROWAVE TIP
Combine the chocolate, butter and water in a bowl. Heat on High for about 1 minute, stirring once, until the chocolate has melted. Finish as above.

CHOCOLATE LIQUEUR SAUCE

75 g / 3 oz plain chocolate or cooking chocolate
10 ml / 2 tsp custard powder or cornflour
15 ml / 1 tbsp orange-flavoured liqueur
15 ml / 1 tbsp caster sugar

Break the chocolate into small pieces and put it in a heatproof bowl with 30 ml / 2 tbsp cold water. Stand the bowl over a saucepan of simmering water and stir until the chocolate melts.

When the chocolate has melted, beat it until smooth, gradually adding 200 ml / 7 fl oz water.

In a cup, mix the custard powder or cornflour with 30 ml / 2 tbsp water, then stir into the chocolate sauce and cook for 3–4 minutes. Stir in the liqueur and the sugar.

MAKES ABOUT 400 ml / 14 fl oz

MOCHA SAUCE

100 g / 4 oz plain chocolate
200 g / 7 oz sugar
125 ml / 4 fl oz strong black coffee
pinch of salt
2.5 ml / ½ tsp vanilla essence

Break up the chocolate and put it into a saucepan with the other ingredients. Stir over gentle heat until the chocolate and sugar melt and the mixture becomes smooth.

Serve hot over ice cream, profiteroles or stewed pears.

MAKES ABOUT 150 ml / ¼ pint

RUM AND RAISIN
CHOCOLATE SAUCE

25 g / 1 oz cocoa
25 g / 1 oz cornflour
25 g / 1 oz caster sugar
450 ml / ¾ pint milk
50 g / 2 oz seedless raisins, chopped
30–45 ml / 2–3 tbsp rum
30–45 ml / 2–3 tbsp single cream

In a bowl, mix the cocoa, cornflour and sugar to a smooth paste with a little of the milk. Heat the rest of the milk until boiling. Stir it into the cocoa paste.

Return the mixture to the saucepan and stir until boiling; simmer for 3 minutes. Remove from the heat and stir in the raisins, rum and cream. Serve the sauce hot or cold.

MAKES ABOUT 250 ml / 8 fl oz

BUTTERSCOTCH SAUCE

1 x 410 g / 14 oz can evaporated milk
100 g / 4 oz soft light brown sugar
100 g / 4 oz caster sugar
50 g / 2 oz butter
15 ml / 1 tbsp clear honey
2.5 ml / ½ tsp vanilla essence
pinch of salt

Put the evaporated milk, sugars, butter, and honey into a heavy-bottomed saucepan. Stir over gentle heat until the sugar has dissolved. Stir in the vanilla essence and salt. Pour into a jug and serve hot with steamed puddings.

MAKES ABOUT 500 ml / 17 fl oz

RICH CHOCOLATE SAUCE

Plain ice cream becomes a party treat with this wickedly rich sauce.

350 g / 12 oz bitter-sweet dessert chocolate, roughly grated
45 ml / 3 tbsp butter
30 ml / 2 tbsp double cream
5 ml / 1 tsp whisky

Put the grated chocolate in a saucepan with 200 ml / 7 fl oz water. Heat gently, stirring all the time, until the chocolate melts. Do not let the sauce boil. Add the butter, 5 ml / 1 tsp at a time, and continue stirring until it melts. Remove the sauce from the heat and stir in the cream and whisky. Serve at once.

MAKES ABOUT 500 ml / 17 fl oz

FREEZER TIP

The sauce may be poured into a heatproof container with a lid, cooled quickly and then frozen for up to 3 months. To use, thaw for 4 hours at room temperature, then stand the container in a saucepan of very hot water until warm.

MARMALADE AND WINE SAUCE

Baked puddings can be somewhat dry.
This zesty sauce is the perfect accompaniment.

90 ml / 6 tbsp orange marmalade
90 ml / 6 tbsp white wine

Combine the marmalade and wine in a saucepan and heat gently for 5 minutes. Transfer to a jug and serve at once.

MAKES ABOUT 175 ml / 6 fl oz

GINGER SYRUP SAUCE

Warm a winter's evening with this sauce
poured over Ginger Pudding (page 175).

strip of lemon rind
piece of fresh root ginger
125 ml / 4 fl oz ginger syrup (from jar of
preserved ginger)
100 g / 4 oz soft light brown sugar, golden syrup or honey
5 ml / 1 tsp lemon juice
10 ml / 2 tsp arrowroot
2.5 ml / ½ tsp ground ginger
15 ml / 1 tbsp preserved ginger, chopped

Put the lemon rind, root ginger and syrup into a saucepan. Add 125 ml / 4 fl oz water. Heat to boiling point. Lower the heat and simmer gently for 15 minutes.

Remove the lemon rind and root ginger. Add the brown sugar, syrup or honey, bring the mixture to the boil and boil for 5 minutes. Stir in the lemon juice.

In a cup, mix the arrowroot and ground ginger with a little cold water until smooth. Stir the arrowroot mixture into the hot liquid. Heat gently until the liquid thickens, stirring all the time.

Add the preserved ginger to the sauce and simmer for 2–3 minutes. Serve hot.

MAKES ABOUT 300 ml / ½ pint

MRS BEETON'S TIP

The syrup in a jar of preserved
ginger makes a delicious addition
to gingerbreads, steamed puddings
and pancakes.

JAM SAUCE

Simple sauces can be highly successful.
Try Jam Sauce on steamed or baked puddings.

60 ml / 4 tbsp seedless jam
lemon juice
10 ml / 2 tsp arrowroot
few drops of food colouring (optional)

Put the jam in a saucepan with 250 ml / 8 fl oz water and bring to the boil. Add lemon juice to taste.

In a cup, mix the arrowroot with a little cold water until smooth. Stir into the hot liquid and heat gently until the sauce thickens, stirring all the time. Add a little colouring if necessary. Pour into a jug and serve at once.

MAKES ABOUT 300 ml / 1 pint

VARIATION

• **Marmalade Sauce** Substitute marmalade for jam and use orange juice instead of water.

SWEET SHERRY SAUCE

75 ml / 5 tbsp sherry
30 ml / 2 tbsp seedless jam or jelly lemon juice

Combine the sherry and jam in a saucepan. Add 75 ml / 5 tbsp water with lemon juice to taste. Bring to the boil and boil for 2–3 minutes. Strain, if necessary, before serving in a jug or sauceboat.

MAKES ABOUT 150 ml / ¼ pint

SWEET BUTTERS

Sweet butters may be used to top pancakes, waffles, crumpets or drop scones. They are also used on fruit puddings, the best example being brandy butter, which is traditionally served with Christmas pudding.

BRANDY BUTTER

50 g / 2 oz butter
100 g / 4 oz caster sugar
15–30 ml / 1–2 tbsp brandy

In a bowl, cream the butter until soft. Gradually beat in the sugar until the mixture is pale and light. Work in the brandy, a little at a time, taking care not to allow the mixture to curdle. Chill before using. If the mixture has separated slightly after standing, beat well before serving.

MAKES ABOUT 150 g / 5 oz

VARIATIONS

- **Sherry Butter** Make as for Brandy Butter but substitute sherry for the brandy. Add a stiffly beaten egg white, if a softer texture is preferred.
- **Vanilla Butter** Make as for Brandy Butter but substitute 5 ml / 1 tsp vanilla essence for the brandy.
- **Orange or Lemon Butter** Cream the grated rind of 1 orange or ½ lemon with the butter and sugar. then gradually beat in 15 ml / 1 tbsp orange juice or 5 ml / 1 tsp lemon juice. Omit the brandy.

BRANDY AND ALMOND BUTTER

100 g / 4 oz unsalted butter
75 g / 3 oz icing sugar
25 g / 1 oz ground almonds
30 ml / 2 tbsp brandy
few drops of lemon juice

In a mixing bowl, cream the butter until very light. Sift in the icing sugar, a little at a time, and beat in each addition lightly but throughly with a fork. Add the almonds in the same way. Lift the fork when beating to incorporate as much air as possible.

Beat in the brandy and lemon juice, a few drops at a time, taking care not to let the mixture separate. Taste, and add extra brandy if liked.

Pile the mixture into a dish and leave to firm up before serving; or turn lightly into a screw-topped jar and store in a cool place until required. Use within one week, or refrigerate for longer storage. Bring to room temperature before serving.

MAKES ABOUT 225 g / 8 oz

RUM BUTTER

50 g / 2 oz butter
100 g / 4 oz soft light brown sugar
30 ml / 2 tbsp rum

In a bowl, cream the butter until soft, beating in the sugar gradually. When light and creamy, work in the rum, a little at a time. Chill the butter before using.

MAKES ABOUT 175 g / 6 oz

CUMBERLAND RUM BUTTER

100 g / 4 oz unsalted butter
100 g / 4 oz soft light brown sugar
30 ml / 2 tbsp rum
2.5 ml / ½ tsp grated orange rind
grated nutmeg

Put the butter in a bowl and cream it until very soft and light-coloured. Crush any lumps in the sugar. Work it into the butter until completely blended in.

Work the rum into the butter, a few drops at a time, take care not to let the mixture separate. Mix in the orange rind. Taste and add a little grated nutmeg.

Pile the rum butter into a dish, and leave to firm up before serving; or turn lightly into a screw-topped jar and store in a cool place until required. Use within 4 days, or refrigerate for longer storage. Bring to room temperature before serving.

MAKES ABOUT 225 g / 8 oz

ORANGE LIQUEUR BUTTER

grated rind of 2 oranges
4 sugar lumps
150 g / 5 oz butter, softened
25 g / 1 oz caster sugar
15 ml / 1 tbsp orange juice, strained
20 ml / 4 tsp Cointreau

Put the orange rind in a bowl and mix it with the sugar lumps. Work in the butter and caster sugar until well blended.

Stir in the juice and liqueur gradually, until fully absorbed. Use at once, or pot and chill as for Almond Butter (page 240).

MAKES ABOUT 175 g / 6 oz

ALMOND BUTTER

100 g / 4 oz butter, softened
100 g / 4 oz ground almonds
about 30 ml / 2 tbsp caster sugar
2.5–5 ml / ½–1 tsp lemon juice
few drops of almond essence

Put the butter in a mixing bowl and work in the ground almonds thoroughly. Add the sugar, lemon juice and almond essence gradually. Use at once or pot (see Mrs Beeton's Tip) and chill.

MAKES ABOUT 225 g / 8 oz

MRS BEETON'S TIP

Pots of Almond Butter make good gifts. Press the butter into small pots or cartons (mini yogurt pots are perfect) and cover. Chill in the refrigerator. Do not freeze.

CHESTNUT BUTTER

200 g / 7 oz unsweetened chestnut purée
200 g / 7 oz butter, softened
30–45 ml / 2–3 tsp caster sugar
15–30 ml / 1–2 tbsp rum

Combine the chestnut purée and butter in a bowl and mix until thoroughly blended. Add the sugar and rum gradually, adjusting the flavour to taste. Chill until firm, then use at once, or pot and chill as for Almond Butter (above).

MAKES ABOUT 450 g / 1 lb

FAIRY BUTTER

Not a whipped butter, but a rich dessert composed
of orange-flavoured strands. It looks very attractive
and may also be used instead of whipped cream
as a topping on a trifle or gâteau.

2 hard-boiled egg yolks
10 ml / 2 tsp orange juice, strained
10 ml / 2 tsp orange flower water
25 g / 1 oz icing sugar, sifted
100 g / 4 oz butter, softened
10 ml / 2 tsp grated orange rind, to decorate

Sieve the egg yolks into a bowl. Using an electric whisk or rotary beater, gradually add the juice, orange flower water, sugar and butter until all the ingredients form a smooth paste.

To use, press the fairy butter through a sieve on to a decorative serving plate or individual plates in a pile of thin strands. Sprinkle with grated orange rind and serve at once.

MAKES ABOUT 175 g / 6 oz

MRS BEETON'S TIP

The pile of butter strands should not
be pressed down. Flick any stray
strands into place with a fork.

Useful Weights and Measures

USING METRIC OR IMPERIAL MEASURES

Throughout the book, all weights and measures are given first in metric, then in imperial. For example 100 g / 4 oz, 150 ml/ ¼ pint or 15 ml / 1 tbsp.

When following any of the recipes use either metric or imperial – do not combine the two sets of measures as they are approximate equivalents, not interchangeable.

EQUIVALENT METRIC / IMPERIAL MEASURES

Weights The following chart lists some of the metric / imperial weights that are used in the recipes.

METRIC	IMPERIAL	METRIC	IMPERIAL
15 g	½ oz	375 g	13 oz
25 g	1 oz	400 g	14 oz
50 g	2 oz	425 g	15 oz
75 g	3 oz	450 g	1 lb
100 g	4 oz	575 g	1¼ lb
150 g	5 oz	675 g	1½ lb
175 g	6 oz	800 g	1¾ lb
200 g	7 oz	900 g	2 lb
225 g	8 oz	1 kg	2¼ lb
250 g	9 oz	1.4 kg	3 lb
275 g	10 oz	1.6 kg	3½ lb
300 g	11 oz	1.8 kg	4 lb
350 g	12 oz	2.25 kg	5 lb

Liquid Measures The following chart lists some metric / imperial equivalents for liquids. Millilitres (ml), litres and fluid ounces (fl oz) or pints are used throughout.

METRIC	IMPERIAL
50 ml	2 fl oz
125 ml	4 fl oz
150 ml	¼ pint
300 ml	½ pint
450 ml	¾ pint
600 ml	1 pint

Spoon Measures Both metric and imperial equivalents are given for all spoon measures, expressed as millilitres and teaspoons (tsp) or tablespoons (tbsp).

All spoon measures refer to British standard measuring spoons and the quantities given are always for level spoons.

Do not use ordinary kitchen cutlery instead of proper measuring spoons as they will hold quite different quantities.

METRIC	IMPERIAL
1.25 ml	¼ tsp
2.5 ml	½ tsp
5 ml	1 tsp
15 ml	1 tbsp

Length All linear measures are expressed in millimetres (mm), centimetres (cm) or metres (m) and inches or feet. The following list gives examples of typical conversions.

METRIC	IMPERIAL
5 mm	¼ inch
1 cm	½ inch
2.5 cm	1 inch
5 cm	2 inches
15 cm	6 inches
30 cm	12 inches (1 foot)

MICROWAVE INFORMATION

Occasional microwave hints and instructions are included for certain recipes, as appropriate. The information given is for microwave ovens rated at 650–700 watts.

The following terms have been used for the microwave settings: High, Medium, Defrost and Low. For each setting, the power input is as follows: High = 100% power, Medium = 50% power, Defrost = 30% power and Low = 20% power.

All microwave notes and timings are for guidance only: always read and follow the manufacturer's instructions for your particular appliance. Remember to avoid putting any metal in the microwave and never operate the microwave empty.

Be very careful when heating liquids in the microwave as they can 'superheat'; i.e. the liquid's surface looks still but underneath there can be boiling bubbles that explode when the container is moved.

OVEN TEMPERATURES

Whenever the oven is used, the required setting is given as three alternatives: degrees Celsius (°C), degrees Fahrenheit (°F) and gas.

The temperature settings given are for conventional ovens. If you have a fan oven, adjust the temperature according to the manufacturer's instructions.

°C	°F	GAS
110	225	¼
120	250	½
140	275	1
150	300	2
160	325	3
180	350	4
190	375	5
200	400	6
220	425	7
230	450	8
240	475	9

Index